Walking Free
The Autobiography of John Edwards

A Walking Free Publication

First published in 2005 with
amendments in 2006, 2008 and 2010

Walking Free

**The Barn
Oakbank Farm
Childs Lane
Wrose
Shipley
BD18 1PA**

http://www.walkingfree.org

British Library Cataloguing in Publication Data.
A catalogue record of this book
is available from the British Library.

ISBN 0 9549400 0 8

Printed and bound in Great Britain by Cox &Wyman Ltd, Reading.

Aknowledgements

I thank God for setting me free. Thank you mam, dad, Pauline, Evelyn, Maeve, Geraldine, Eamon and Michael for giving me so many chances and for waiting for me. Thank you to my beautiful wife Tricia for your patience and love as I put my pain on paper. I love you more and more.

Thank you Gary and Wilma for your obedience to God. Thanks to all the men at FGBMFI Dublin. You know who you are. Thanks to Alan, Jean, Sarah, Niamh, Aisling and Ian. I'm sure your mam is cheering us on.

Thank you Shay, my faithful friend, for your patience with me as you corrected and proof-read my efforts. You're simply the best friend in the world.

Thanks John and Ann Macey, Pastor Hughes, Gareth Cheedy, The Cundills, Jay Fallon for being there when I needed him, and David and Beryl Ware my dear friends in Wales. Thanks to all my friends in St Mark's, Dublin.

Foreword

This is a story that had to be written.

Finally, after nearly twenty years, my friend John has put pen to paper and shared his life's testimony with us – and what a story! Born into a middle-class family on Dublin's north side, it would have seemed initially that every opportunity was available for John to succeed in life. Yet forces that were beyond his control conspired with a litany of difficulties to undermine John's confidence in himself and in life in general.

The John I met in St Mark's church, seventeen years ago, was emaciated by years of drug and alcohol abuse and full of fear of rejection as he sought for yet another answer to his myriad personal difficulties. The journey that we walked over the next four years was tortuous beyond belief, an emotional rollercoaster that saw him one moment free and the next one tripped-up again by his inability to make the right choices. Yet slowly, painfully, John began to change. A new hope was born through a life-changing encounter with our Lord Jesus Christ. With the support of a community of faith, his family and John's personal stubborn belief that his life wasn't destined to end in a dark alleyway with a needle in his arm, change began to occur.

You need to read this story and then pass it on to a friend who might be challenged by it. It is a story of hope in the face of hopelessness, faith in spite of failure and a God-given determination to succeed when it seems everything is against you.

This story will make you laugh out loud, wipe an inadvertent tear from your eye and cause you to reflect on the power of love and forgiveness. Like John, you too can turn your trials into triumphs, your hurts into halos and your scars into stars.

Pastor Gary Davidson

A word from Moya Brennan (the Voice of Clannad)

The first time I met John I was blown away hearing his story and how his life was turned around in such an incredible way. It showed me that you can never be so far down that God will fail to reach you.

I was so impressed with the commitment that had come from God touching John's heart and that he would dedicate his whole life in reaching out to those who had walked a similar path. I'm thrilled that he has, at last, written his story so that others can enjoy – with laughter and tears – the experiences that have made him what he is today.

My family and I have been honoured to know John and Tricia. They have inspired our lives, and this book will inspire yours.

Author's Note

Out of consideration for friends and families I have, in some instances, changed the names of persons mentioned in 'Walking Free'.

Contents

*I dedicate this book to the memory of my Dad,
Eddie Edwards. You would be proud of me now, Da.*

I miss you at moments like this.

*I also dedicate this book to the Mams,
Dads and families of the still-suffering addict.*

Keep on hoping, keep on praying.

Chapter One
In the Beginning

"Hey, my Irish amigo, want some more coffee?" Art asked.

"Yes, please," I answered, lifting my eyes to look down the table at him. Candles flickered everywhere, casting shadows across his tanned face; he was smiling, white teeth shining from under a huge Mexican moustache. The atmosphere was friendly; a guitarist played beautiful Mexican music while he sang softly in Spanish. I was enjoying the company of some fascinating people in a plush, Mexican restaurant near Hollywood in Los Angeles. It was my first time to meet some of them. We had a lot in common: dark but different histories and a similar destiny. Here, tonight, we were meeting together to laugh, cry and share our wonder at the way in which our paths had crossed. I looked around the table at the company I was in: Ernest Kilroy, a man of much influence in the Mexican Mafia, who had spent many years in prison; his wife Rosa; Blinkey Rodriguez, ex-kickboxing champion of California and his wife Anna, female kickboxing champion of Orange County. Then there was Art, who had been an assassin with the Mexican Mafia, a man that was until recently feared by all. He had not long come out of death row in San Quentin Prison.

"Hey, John, tell Ernest about the night you nearly got arrested by the Queen's police when you stayed at her Balmoral estate in Scotland."

Everyone listened intently to me and laughed with me as I related the story of my stay at Balmoral and how I almost got arrested by the Queen's police. These people respected me and

1

gladly accepted me into their company. I felt safe with them, protected, and confident. Blinkey then told a funny story about his kickboxing club. I began to think about Dublin in Ireland, my mam and dad and the difficult road I had walked for most of my life. The music drifted into the distance as my mind went back over my life; I recalled many incidents that had led me to this present gathering. It had been a tough road and I was lucky to be alive – or was it luck? It had seemed to me that right from the day I was born, fate had it in for me. Fate failed to consider, though, that I was a fighter that didn't know how to give in.

On the night of 7th December 1954, Annesley Bridge on the Tolka River burst open and there was a great flood all through the North Strand and Fairview, the suburb of Dublin close to where my family lived. Perhaps that was a sign of things ahead; a forewarning of how turbulent the course of my life would become. Yet it didn't alarm my family very much; for them this was a night of joyful anticipation, culminating in an event that not even the flooded streets could dampen. For at two o'clock in the morning providence brought them a baby boy – none other than I, John Edwards.

My parents were already blessed with four girls; they had always wanted a boy and now this longing had been fulfilled. Mr and Mrs Edwards were more proud than ever in their lives before.

My dad visited the Rotunda hospital the day after I was born.

"How are they?" he asked a nurse as he entered the maternity wing that my mother was in.

"Mother and baby are well," the nurse replied. My dad raced past her, but he paused momentarily to compose himself before running to my mam's bedside. She was cradling me in her arms.

"It's a boy, Eddie," she said with pride in her eyes. "It's a boy, and he weighs eleven pounds. And just look at his dimples." My dad, who was normally a quiet man and very composed, completely forgot himself and danced around the maternity wing singing a happy song with me in his arms.

IN THE BEGINNING

"Stop it, Eddie – you'll have the whole ward talking about us!"

"I don't care," my dad said. "This is one of the happiest days of my life." Then he remembered his gift for my mam. Picking up his briefcase he took out a beautifully wrapped package. "Here you are, Alice – a lovely bottle of Emu wine for a great mother and wife. I love you, darling," he whispered. "Thank you for a wonderful baby boy."

Both mother and baby were well and were expected home in about a week. Pauline, Evelyn, Maeve, and Geraldine helped their father prepare the house for our arrival. I was to be called John. When we got home my sisters had everything ready for us. The cot that each of them had once occupied was parked at the side of my parents' bed. The sides were lowered and the lovely soft woollen patchwork and blue baby blankets were in place, ready to receive the first boy of the Edwards family.

That evening my Uncle Tommy and Auntie Eileen visited; then a steady stream of the neighbours called to see "the new baby". Mrs Purcell, Mrs Kelly, Mrs Rogers and Mrs Lounds all came in.

"Oh Alice, he's a beautiful baby and just look at the size of him."

"He looks about three months old and his dimples are gorgeous."

"He must have been a hard baby to give birth to – was he, Alice?"

"It took me two hours just to deliver his head," my ma said.

"Oh my God, you poor thing!" they all cried in unison.

"And I haven't even got one stitch," my ma said with pride.

"Alice, you're amazin'!" they all agreed. My uncle Tommy was listening in on this conversation and he commented: "He's going to be huge when he grows up – probably be a great Gaelic football player or hurler."

"What are you going to call him, Alice?" asked Mrs Lounds, our next-door neighbour.

"John Charles," my ma said, "after the Archbishop of Dublin."

"Oh! Very nice," said Mrs Lounds, with a distant look in her eyes (she was a Protestant). Mrs O'Rourke butted in and said,

"That's a great name for him. Maybe he'll be a priest when he grows up, Alice."

I'm told that everything went well for the first few months of my life. My sisters loved having a little brother. The older ones, Pauline, Evelyn and Maeve, would help my ma by looking after me and giving her a chance to have a rest in the afternoons. They would even take me up to their friends' houses sometimes and bring me for short walks, pushing me along in the big grey pram.

When I was six months old I began to get a wheeze in my chest. This quickly changed to a bad cough and a cold. My ma nursed me as well as she could but in no time at all I had developed pneumonia. The doctor felt it was best to keep me at home. Many times my mother thought that I was going to die. Everyone was having Masses said for me, from the Carmelites to the Capuchins; there were Masses being said on my behalf in St Gabrielle's and St John's Church and the church in Killester, and all my cousins around the country were praying for me. The nuns down in the local convent prayed daily for me, and even Father Mangen prayed for me. He was a real holy man and he was the parish priest as well, so I was in with a good chance.

As it happened, I came through that sickness quite successfully, but I had lost a lot of weight and I was never a big baby after it. My growth seemed to slow right down and many of the other kids around the Grove where we lived passed me by, at least as far as physical size was concerned. Uncle Tommy began to think that maybe I would make a good jockey and not a hurler or football player after all.

Starting School

My best friend was Kevin. He lived in the fourth house down the road from ours. Kevin and me did everything together.

On our first day in school my ma and Kevin's ma brought us down to Belgrove School on Seafield Road in Clontarf. The boys used to start school in the girls' section then, in classes set apart for small boys.

I'll never forget that first terrible day in Belgrove. I was terrified, and so was Kevin; we couldn't even comfort each other, we were so frightened. I hadn't slept very well the night before. We set off from the house at about 8.30 a.m. I had my new brown leather school bag hung on my back, with my new pencils, my pen with a nib and my jotters all tucked away inside. But the most important thing in the bag was my lunch. My ma had made some lovely sandwiches, and there was an apple as well. We walked up to the bus stop with Mrs Purcell and Kevin. We got the 44a bus outside Manresa, the big Jesuit house, and we were down at the school in about ten minutes. It was a big, old, spooky building. I can remember that we stood just inside the front door at the bottom of an enormous staircase with what seemed like about 200 other children. Our mothers stood by our sides holding our hands. They too were sad because their little boys were growing up. My eyes were fixed on the stairs; I was looking up to where they disappeared around a corner. I was waiting for the appearance of Mrs Cannon, the headmistress, or "Cannonballs" as my sisters called her. She was reputed to be an awful thing, "a huge oul' one" my sister said she was, and she was always shouting at you, and she had red hair, and *loads* of make-up.

Eventually I heard the sound of footsteps coming from the corridor on the upper floor.

"This must be her," I thought, as I braced myself to catch my first glimpse of this giant of my fears. Then all of a sudden – there she was at the top of the stairs. All us kids were looking up at her with eyes wide and mouths open, holding our breath and our mothers' hands tightly, afraid to let go. My worst fears were embodied in this woman; she was everything I dreaded and more; her hair was up in a bun and her piercing eyes were looking right through us. I was determined not to cry, but as Cannonballs put us through our paces and then separated us from our mothers to go to our different classes everyone except Kevin and me were in tears. We were brave for the whole day. Funny thing is, our mothers cried.

We went into Mrs Molloy's class. Eighty of us were to be taught by her. She was lovely and she made us feel at home.

Every morning my mother would give me a lunch to bring to school. It usually consisted of jam or marmalade sandwiches, packed in the wrapper from a Johnston, Mooney & O'Brien sliced pan, and a salad-cream bottle filled with milk.

"Don't forget to bring your paper and the bottle home with you," she would say to us as we left to get the bus. Every Friday she gave us a penny for the "black babies" who were dying of hunger somewhere in the world. We were often reminded of those black babies, especially when we wouldn't eat our dinner. "Just think of them black babies starving to death and you not even eating a dinner that's cooked for you at home." Then with terrible feelings of guilt and vivid images of crying, starving black babies in our little minds we would cram as much food into ourselves as we possibly could.

Another Child is Born

One day all my sisters and I were sitting in the dining room having tea at the big, red-topped table, when my mother made an announcement to us.

"Kids," she said, "guess what?"

We all stopped eating and looked intently at her. We knew by the way she spoke that she had something really important to say to us. She waited till she had our full attention and then said with a big smile on her face, "In six months time, I'm going to have a baby." She stuck her tummy out and patted it as she told us. All the girls jumped up and surrounded her, hugging her and feeling her tummy, wondering aloud if the baby would be a boy or a girl.

"What are you going to call it, ma?" one of them asked.

"When is it due?" asked someone else. There was great glee and anticipation in the Edwards household that evening. I didn't get unduly excited – in fact I took it all in my stride. My da came in later from the pub and he sat down in his chair with his six large bottles of Guinness. The girls didn't get as excited around him as they had with my ma, because he was in one of his serious moods. Yet he was happy that my mother was going to have another baby.

The six remaining months of her pregnancy passed quickly. Then one Saturday my da was about to go down to the Dollymount Inn for a pint when my mother said, "Eddie, I think that you better bring me into the Rotunda hospital. I'm feeling a lot of pressure and I'm afraid if you go out I might go into labour before you get back."

My da always insisted that my ma went as a private patient so as to get the best attention. As soon as she had arrived in the hospital the nurse examined her and told her that she was about to have the baby.

"You better wait for Doctor Cross, Mrs Edwards, before you start pushing." Doctor Cross wouldn't have got his fifty pounds if he missed the birth.

"I could have had the baby there and then," my ma told us later, "but I had to wait ten minutes for the doctor."

"Hold on now, Mrs Edwards," the nurses said, "he'll be here in a minute or two." He finally arrived and he wasn't in the door ten seconds when my little brother shot like a cork out of a bottle into the world. "That must have been the easiest fifty quid that Doctor Cross ever earned," my ma said.

Back in the house my sisters were doing their bit again, preparing the cot with the lovely soft blankets and arranging everything for the baby's homecoming. Uncle Tommy, Auntie Eileen, Mrs Lounds and the other neighbours were informed of my mother's and the new baby's return. They readied themselves for the welcome home and to see the baby's visitors.

The new baby was called Eamon, Gaelic for Edward. Everyone was giving him loads of attention.

"Oh what lovely brown eyes he has and isn't he so cute!"

"He'll probably be a hurler or a Gaelic football player," my Uncle Tommy said hopefully.

I found myself becoming quite jealous of the new arrival. I was the one who usually got all the attention but now Eamon was the man of the moment.

"Be careful of the soft spot on the top of the baby's head, John," my ma said to me.

"I will, ma." Then when nobody was looking, I would smack Eamon on the very soft spot that I had been warned not to touch.

One day when he was about three years of age and I was about seven, I decided that I had had enough of my little brother.

"That's it! I'm fed up with him – I'm going to kill him." I took hold of him and dragged him outside and down the road, stopping outside Mr Rodger's house. I then started to beat Eamon up with my fists. Eamon spoiled my plan by screaming so loudly that the whole neighbourhood could hear him.

"Shut up, Eamon, you'll get me in trouble," I cried, beginning to panic. At that moment Mr Rodgers came running out of his house, shouting, "Leave him alone, John Edwards or I'm telling your mother." I ran away and hid down the end of the park behind a tree. I decided that I would try to get on with Eamon instead of killing him, as I would get into less trouble that way. I'm happy to say that my relationship with Eamon greatly improved from that point. Mr Rodgers must have kept the incident quiet because my ma never said a word to me about it.

Just when I had accepted Eamon and begun to really appreciate him as a brother my ma announced that she was pregnant again. This time she had another little boy, Michael, who was blonde and blue-eyed and everyone loved him. I'm happy to say that I didn't get jealous this time. I accepted Michael from the word go and treated him well. In fact, I began to appreciate having two little brothers.

Chapter Two
A Good Time Had by All

The Park

One of my earliest memories is of playing with my pals on the elm trees, out in the field in Mount Prospect Grove in Clontarf. Everyone called this field "the park". It was about one-and-a-half acres in size and was rectangular in shape. When I was very young there were tennis courts at one end of it. Our house was situated on the west side of the park, about two lampposts down.

The tree we most often played on was the "Mailer", so called because if you climbed to the top of the tree (over 100 feet) you could see the mail-boat going out to Liverpool at eight o'clock each night. My best friend Kevin and I played there almost every night, along with the rest of the gang. We would climb up to the very top and then rest on the branches, lying stretched out on them. We were totally unconcerned about the height or the danger. If our mothers were in their gardens or if our fathers were coming along the road on the way back from work we would shout down to them, "Hey ma – da – can you see me?" Then once we had their attention we would scale out onto the end of the highest branch we could reach and clamber along it until it bent so much that it touched the branch below. Then to the horror of our parents we would let go of the top branch and attach ourselves to the lower branch, screeching with delight as we did so.

"You be careful up there, John Edwards!" my parents shouted. We would scale all the way down the tree until we reached the two big branches that held our tree hut. This was a platform made of bits of wood nailed onto two big branches about fifteen feet from the base of the tree. We had a swing attached to this branch, which provided literally years of fun for all generations of kids in the Grove. I was always grateful for the freedom my parents gave us kids in our sometimes limb-risking games; it gave us courage, and bred a confidence in us for dealing with dangerous situations.

This tree was a place for dreaming and learning. We usually sat on the highest branches in the section we called "the lounge". As many as five or six of us gathered up there sometimes. We would look out over the houses in the Grove and see the ships going to foreign lands. There was Kevin and me, with Robert O'Rourke, Kev and Ritchie Lynch, and sometimes John Slye.

John was a Protestant and we were all Catholics. He was always better dressed than we were, and his house was painted nicer than any of our homes. The Protestants on our road had fewer brothers and sisters than we had. They attended Greenlanes School, while all the Catholics went to Belgrove School. We liked John in spite of those differences and he hung around with us now and again. Paddy and Gerry Tracy were our constant companions also. We called ourselves the "Jinx Gang"; Kevin was Jinx and was the gang leader while I was the "second in charge" because I was the fastest runner in the school. We would all sit up on top of the Mailer tree and talk about doing great things some day, or travelling to foreign places – desert islands, perhaps, or even London – or maybe joining our cousins in America and other parts of the world.

One day John Slye came up and told us about a very strange thing that men and women get up to. The "birds and the bees", he called it, and the act was called intercourse.

"How do you know this is true?" I asked him.

"Me da told me," he said.

I said, "That sounds awful, I'll never do that." The gang and me were amazed at this news and we made John swear that he would find out more for us about this terrible thing called intercourse.

The next week he came back with a terrifying story of a

couple he was told about that got stuck together while practising intercourse. Amazed we asked, "How did they get separated?"

"They had to go to hospital," John said. We all agreed as a gang that day that we would never, ever, do that awful thing.

Hare Island

My da was the best da in the world as far as I was concerned and I loved being with him. He was my hero. I always tried to please him. He had the best job on the road and he earned more money than anyone else did, too. I knew this was true because Robbie O'Rourke's da had told him. Robbie's da was a tailor near Grafton Street and he was rich; he used to make my da's suits and if he said my da was rich – well, it must be true. I was delighted my da was rich and I was so proud of him.

He used to bring us on great holidays. Some years he rented an island in Lough Ree on the river Shannon near Athlone. My ma, my four sisters, my two brothers and me would go over together with my Uncle Podge and my Auntie Heather and their two kids. We drove to Cuson Point near Athlone in our Vauxhall Cresta and there we would get on board a big grey clinker-built rowing boat. This belonged to Paddy Duffy, who also owned the island. We would all pile in with food, clothes and kids and row the half-mile to "our Island".

Here we stayed in a large old house, situated right in the centre of the island. It had no electricity, but instead we used gaslights and a big old solid fuel-burning range. For heating we lit a lovely turf fire. There were potties under the beds for peeing in during the night.

Late at night my da and Uncle Podge used to sneak back onto the mainland to collect a couple of barrels of Guinness that they had hidden in some bushes at Cuson Point before we rowed over in the boat. Mr Duffy, who owned the island, didn't like drink so they had to smuggle it in. Great excitement accompanied the arrival of the Guinness. Once it was dark the entire family would make our way down to the little pier to watch for the two smugglers' return. It was a great adventure; all of us would be nervous in case Mr Duffy might have stayed on the island that night. If he caught us with drink there would be blue murder. Every now and again one or more of us would burst out in nervous laughter.

"Shut up, John," my ma would say if I laughed.

"Sorry, ma, I can't help it."

"There'll be hell to pay if Mr Duffy hears you." This only had the effect of making us laugh all the more. My da had said that if Mr Duffy saw the Guinness he would kick us off the island, so we were all obliged to keep it a secret. Once we were down by the pier we would huddle together in a group and listen for the sound of my da's or Uncle Podge's voice travelling over the water or the sound of wooden oars parting the waves or hitting against the side of the boat.

"Are ye there, kids?" my da would say as the boat got near.

"Yes, da, we're all here."

"Tie the boat up against the pier for us while we take the barrels of Guinness off."

Great grunts and groans were heard as we struggled to get the barrels ashore. Then two wheelbarrows that we had brought with us were loaded with the Guinness and off we went. Each of the kids flanked the Guinness, while keeping a look-out for the enemy (Mr Duffy). Once we arrived at the house the Guinness was placed in the kitchen and a tap was put on one of the barrels. My da and Uncle Podge would then pour a hard-earned pint of Guinness for themselves. We kids were each given a little sample of it to celebrate its arrival.

We had absolutely great fun throughout those holidays. My parents allowed us the freedom to do pretty much what we liked. We went out fishing on the boats with my da and Uncle Podge, and we often caught huge pike and perch. When we brought them home we would put the washing line through their gills and hang them there. My ma and Auntie Heather always gave out to us because the washing-lines were for the baby's nappies. Us men knew that they were really for the fish, though. The women always seemed to get their own way. I never understood that.

Joyfully we chased the turkeys and peacock around the yard and put up any feathers we snatched as trophies on the mantelpiece in the big house. In the evenings we all sat around and sang. My ma and da sang lovely songs together, my da harmonising in a beautiful tenor voice. "Silent Night" was my favourite, even in summer. Then my da would do a tap dance in his leather shoes on the hard floor over in a corner by the window. *Gosh*, I thought, *my da knows everything and he can do everything*. It seemed to me sometimes that he was a ghost because he even knew things I had done that I didn't tell him about. He would say, "A little birdie told me."

There was no television on the island so us kids would make up plays or do TV ads for the adults. The "Johnston, Mooney & O'Brien" TV ad was our favourite. We would put up blankets for stage curtains and dress up. Each of us had lines to say and we would come out from behind the stage curtain to the applause of the adults, who sat drinking their Guinness and having a great time of it. I never used to speak much in the plays if I could help it because I had a stutter. Usually I avoided speaking by taking on the role of stage-manager.

Chapter Three
Troubled Times

My Left Hand

Back in Dublin, I would go out with my dad any chance I got. Sometimes he would announce that he was going for a drive and he would bring me with him, but more and more often he just went as far as the Dollymount Inn, the local pub down by the sea-front. I wasn't allowed into the pub so I would have to sit in the car and wait for him to come out. It was very boring sitting there, sometimes for hours, and I can remember thinking, "It'll be great when I'm eighteen and I can go in and drink with me da and not have to wait out here for him."

Sometimes we would go down along Dollymount beach to play golf at St Anne's Golf Club. On those occasions I was his caddie. Eventually he got a little club made for me and I would try to impress him as I did my best to out-putt or out-drive him. Sometimes I really did succeed in out-putting him and we would have a laugh about it. At this stage I was about eight years old, and my stutter was getting worse.

"W-w-watch me p-p-putt-this one, da."

"Well done, son," he would say, even if I didn't do well. Sometimes I noticed him looking at me with great love and concern. I could see it in his eyes. He had dark eyes, piercing eyes; at times they could be scary, but at other times, if you knew him well, you could see the love in them. Sometimes he would grab me and rub my face with his chin, especially if he hadn't shaved. I loved it when he did that; I could smell him – it wasn't a dirty smell, because he was a very clean man, but my da had a lovely smell: I think it was a mixture of pipe tobacco and Brilliantine hair-oil.

On another occasion we went to the airport with some people from Clontarf Yacht Club. Mr Mackey from the top of our road was a pilot with Aer Lingus and he had arranged for us to go into the control tower to see the radar monitors and meet the air traffic controllers. I noticed that my da was very quiet that day and I was a bit worried about him as he was also very pale. On our way out, he suddenly held onto my shoulder and made a funny, groaning noise. Then he collapsed in a heap on the ground, unconscious. I thought that he was dead. Mr Mackey and some of the others came over and rested his head on a rolled-up carpet. When he came to after a while, we discovered that he had wet himself. I was totally confused. My dad lying in public, unconscious and wetting himself! This was totally foreign to me and I couldn't handle it. None of the other men present paid any attention to me, nor did they realise the trauma I was going through watching my dad in this state. After about half-an-hour he had recovered enough to go home. He was drinking a lot at that time.

There were times when he would give me lectures. I hated those.

"Son," he would say, "I have had a hard time making it in life; I have had to do things the hard way. I didn't go to university like other men. I trained myself and now I am at the top of the motor business in Ireland. You don't have to do it that way, son; you will go to university and be a success. You will not be a road-sweeper or dustbin-man."

My dad did his best to teach me things as a child. He taught me how to play chess. I hated the game but I played it partly to keep him happy but mostly because I liked to be with him and have his attention all to myself. I was left-handed from the time I was born, and this was reckoned to be a bad thing in those days in Ireland. A left-handed person was called a "citog", an Irish word that had evil or superstitious connotations. My father would say, "John, you must learn to use your right hand for writing and I am going to help you."

TROUBLED TIMES

One day he came home from work with a small black rubber ball.

"Here, John," he said, "take this and hold it in your left hand until you learn to use your right hand for everything." I cannot remember this period of my life very well; I seem to have blocked it out; but my sisters tell me that I suffered terribly as my dad relentlessly made me use my right hand. I do remember being put out of the dining room when I would not use my right hand for my knife.

"Stand outside the door until you make your mind up to do as I say, John," my dad said. I would stand outside and cry. Sometimes my mother argued with him over this, and then I would be even more upset.

Big Boys' School

I made my mind up one day that I would try my best to use my right hand. My stutter got steadily worse during this time but I persevered. In the meantime, I suffered terribly in school.

I'll never forget the day I moved into the big boys' school. All the boys were lined up in rows of two and were marched from the baby school into the big boys' premises just down the road. I felt that I was now a grown-up and had it made.

My first teacher in the big school was John McGahern. He was a great teacher, very easy-going, and he made the lessons very interesting. I did well while I was in his class. I guess I felt accepted by him. Sometimes he gave us work to do while he sat up at the front of the class with his feet up on his desk and his hands in his pockets. Then, clearing his throat, he would spit great big golliers out of the open window. "Hope there is nobody downstairs under that," I would say to myself.

The school must have been having cutbacks at the time because we kids used to have to polish the floors. We were allowed to bring in socks, which we put on over our shoes, so that we could slide around the tiles in the corridors and classrooms. We took great pride in the shine on our floor. Every Friday Mr Kellagher the headmaster presented a cup to the class with the shiniest floor. We all worked hard trying to win that cup every week.

17

Life took a turn for the worse when I moved into third class. We heard that Mr McGahern was fired for writing some book or something and I was put into Mr Cleary's class. He was deputy headmaster and he was stern. Kevin and I were separated at this time. He was put in the class next door with Mr Gough. Mr Cleary used the cane a lot and I was frightened of him.

By now my stutter was quite bad and I was terribly self-conscious about it. Sometimes during English class, when we were reading aloud, the teacher would suddenly pick on someone, saying, "Murphy or Edwards, what is the next word?" Usually when he asked me I could not get the word out because of my stutter and because I was frightened. "Come up to the front of the class for the cane, Edwards," he would say. Once as I was walking up towards the front I managed to stutter the word that I had just failed to speak.

"P-p-powerful," I mumbled.

"Somebody prompted you," he said. Nobody had, but I didn't argue with him. I put my hand out and he gave me several of the best with his bamboo cane. On another occasion the same thing happened but this time instead of giving me the cane he made me stand out in the middle of the schoolyard on top of a drain. Everybody could see me there, as the yard was surrounded by classrooms. I had to stand still on this spot until Mr Cleary decided to call me in. I knew that I was guilty of nothing except having a stutter, yet I felt that everyone in the school was looking at me as if I was no good and had been guilty of doing something wrong. I even felt as if I *had* done something bad, and began to develop a guilt complex. Whenever something went wrong in school or anywhere else I would turn bright red as if I was responsible, which inevitably attracted the suspicions of those around me. I would, of course, try to explain myself but with my stutter I found this very difficult.

Mr Cleary often asked me to read out loud in the class, which was something I truly dreaded. I would stutter and stumble my way through it, while the boys in the class laughed at me. They tried to bully me in the yard as well, but even though I was smaller than most of them I put up a good fight. Most times I drew first blood, as a result of which nobody really bullied me too much. Nevertheless, I often went home from school and hid myself in my bedroom, crawling under the bed. I would cry there and ask God to take my stutter away, and to stop me blushing. I would eventually get out from under the bed and look in my wardrobe mirror. I would speak to myself and say things like, "You will not stutter when you go downstairs, you will not blush any more." I could speak beautifully when I was on my own but as soon as I was with someone else I would start stuttering. I couldn't understand this.

My father was determined to break this stutter and he tried every trick in the book to do so. He would get me into our sitting-room and try to teach me to speak in a normal way. If there were a knock on the door I would have to answer it; I would have to find out the person's name and the name of the person he or she was seeking. Then I would have to go to the latter and repeat everything that had been said to me. I hated this ordeal because I would stutter all the way through the whole episode. I was exhausted and completely defeated after each attempt. This didn't help my stutter at all. Then my father began to get me to answer the phone in the house whenever it rang. Again I would have to find out who the call was for and then convey the message. Each time I had to go through this routine I felt worse about myself. I began to fear my dad. Whenever I heard his key in the front door I ran upstairs to hide, my stomach in knots and my whole being full of tension.

I felt the same way about school now as well. Every morning I was sick with worry. I knew exactly where Mr Cleary parked his car and every day without fail I looked out of the window of the bus to see if his little blue Princess car was in its place. If it wasn't there it meant for some reason he wouldn't be in. Once or twice this turned out to be the case and I was absolutely thrilled; the sense of relief was incredible. On such occasions we were put in someone else's class for the day and the pressure was turned off for a while. Unfortunately, he rarely missed a day.

Fear of Man

About this time I began to retreat into myself. I played for hours alone with my Dinky cars or my Scalextric set, losing myself in a dream world of my own invention. I was quite happy there; nobody bothered me and I could talk quite clearly to my imaginary friends as I pushed my little cars down make-believe roads. I invented neighbours and shops with kind shopkeepers who didn't cause me to stutter. I got on famously with all these amazing people, and I even imagined my dad in the game, his car always the biggest car; and he always very kind to me. In my dream world he never made me do things that upset me and he never drank too much. We would drive down to the golf club in those games and play nine holes together. I was really missing him.

My dad began to drink more than ever at this time. He visited the pub on the way home from work and having drunk there he would bring home six large bottles of Guinness. I only saw him drunk a few times and he never hit my ma or any of us children, but sometimes at night when we were in bed I could hear him arguing downstairs. His tongue could hurt you more than Mr Cleary's bamboo cane. I was sharing a double bed with my little brother Eamon at this time. Eamon would begin to get upset when he heard my da shouting at my ma so I used to comfort him and tell him that everything was going to be OK.

"Sure they're not really fightin', Eamon," I'd say, "they're just havin' a loud conversation."

"No they're not," Eamon would say. Then he would begin to cry. I wanted to cry too but I had to be strong for him.

"God," I would pray, "please, please let me lose a leg; let me have an accident, not *too* bad a one, and let me lose a leg." I didn't understand why I prayed this prayer, but I used to pray it with all of my might. I guess I felt that if I wasn't well I would either get the attention that I craved from my da, or else that he would stop fighting my ma.

Sometimes when I couldn't bear the pain of hearing them arguing downstairs I went down in my pyjamas and asked them to stop.

"Please stop arguin'," I would say. "It's upsettin' Eamon."

"Get back up to bed, John, and don't come down again," my da would reply. Then I would go back to bed and lie there, earnestly praying, "God let me lose a leg." I was fearful of every important male adult or authority around me at this time of my life and I was very unhappy.

My Fear of God

One day during this period I was in Gago's field at the back of our houses. Gago was a rich man and he owned a huge house, a lovely Georgian mansion, with about ten bedrooms in it. He had occupied this building with his daughters and some nephews, but now that he was getting older he decided to sell the house and land and build a smaller, more manageable house just down the road. All of us kids used to play in the big house after Gago vacated it. He had left most of the furniture in it – very expensive stuff it was too. We played all kinds of games in there. One day we were playing war, using slings for weapons. Me and the Jinx gang had possession of the house and the fellas from the other side of the Grove were trying to capture it from us. I was defending one of the upstairs rooms, keeping guard over the side of the house, and nobody could get me. For ammunition I had gathered loads of rocks and stones that I could fling at anyone who came near. I could see Allister Stewart trying to sneak up by the side-wall so I flung a load of them at him. He had a big sling but he wasn't a very good shot. The Jinx gang were going to win the house again today. I stuck my head out of the window and said, "Stewarty, you couldn't hit me with that sling if you tried." With that he turned around and, firing a single shot, he hit me right between the eyes with a stone, knocking me out cold. All his pals came storming in the side door and won the house off us that day. I was lucky he didn't kill me. I had a huge cut on my forehead and when I went home my ma put a big bandage on it for me. All the rest of the gang were jealous of my big bandage and my war wound so I was happy as anything for a few days.

A week later we planned to return to Gago's for another war. We were determined to win the house back. The day before the battle I went around on my own to the big house to gather piles of rocks and stones and sticks and anything else that I could find. I was busy doing this when I saw Kevin Joyce from number 42 coming into the house. I was in the front room of the ground floor when he saw me.

"How're ye, John," he said as he walked into the room. "What are ye doin'?"

"Preparing for war," I replied. "We're going to beat Alistair Stewart in the biggest war you ever did see tomorrow. You can help me collect the ammo if you like," I added.

"Great," said Kevin, feeling honoured to be a part of the Jinx gang for a while. "What happened your head?" he asked.

"I got wounded last week trying to hold off the enemy."

"Wow," he said, "you're *real* brave. I bet you would do anything."

"Yeah, 'course I would," I said.

"Would you break that mirror over there?" he asked, pointing to a huge five-by-four-foot mirror that was mounted in a beautiful carved wooden frame and hinged on a lovely carved wooden base. None of the gang had ever touched this because we knew it was worth a lot of money.

"I dare you," he said.

"Na, I don't want to get glass on the ground, someone might get injured in the battle tomorrow," I said. This didn't silence Kevin though.

"I double dare you," he said. "Look – here's an old alarm clock that you can use to smash it with." So saying, he handed me an old blue, rusty, wind-up alarm clock. I was put on the spot, and not wanting to look bad or have a bad report spread around about me, I stuttered and stumbled trying to find a way out of breaking this lovely mirror. When I couldn't find an excuse to avoid the challenge I finally gave in and said, "Okay, I'll do it." Inside my head I thought, "What have I done, I've committed myself." I knew that I was now doing something that I didn't want to do and I hated the predicament I had put myself in. I had no choice but to do it now. With that, I slowly reached out my arm, took hold of the alarm clock and aimed it with minimum force at one of the corners of the mirror, hoping that if I didn't throw it too hard the glass might not break. The old alarm clock appeared to sail in slow motion as it tumbled and flew through the air towards the mirror. I held my breath as it travelled the last few inches before hitting the glass, time itself seeming to slow down. I could see both Kevin's reflection and my own in the mirror. We were standing staring with our mouths open.

"Maybe it won't break," I thought, without saying anything. Then with a "crunch" the clock hit the glass and the mirror was smashed in a thousand pieces. The glass seemed to make the loudest noise imaginable as it crashed to the floor.

"Oh no!" I thought, "I'm for it now."

"You're crazy!" Kevin shouted at me as he ran from the house as fast as he could. I was right behind him, running straight across the field, through the hole in the fence, and down the lane that went around behind our houses. My thoughts too were racing. "Oh! God, what have I done! – If I get caught for this I'm going to be in the biggest trouble ever!"

Suddenly I heard a voice calling me. "John, come back here." It was my da.

"He's definitely a ghost," I thought, "he knows every time I do something wrong. – Oh! Me life is over."

I stopped running and went back to him, ready to confess everything.

"How're ye, da," I said, waiting for the tongue-lashing that this time I knew I deserved.

"What are you running for, John?" he said. "Your mam is out in the car, we've been looking everywhere for you. We're going into town to buy you a new pair of shoes in Cleary's. Hurry up now and let's go."

I felt sure that he knew I had done something wrong; guilt was written all over my face. I sat in the back of the car and thought about what I had done to the mirror. It was lucky that he hadn't found out. Then it struck me that I had probably committed a mortal sin. We had been learning about what a mortal sin was in school and I was sure that so far, that is until today, I had never committed one. Now I had really done it. I believed in God and I prayed to him every night, but this time I had committed a sin that I thought could not be forgiven. I had been taught in school that there are two kinds of sins, venial sins and mortal sins. My understanding of it was that if you died with venial sins you would go to purgatory for a long time, possibly thousands of years, until you got purged of them. We used to pray regularly in school and at Mass for these poor souls in purgatory. One of our teachers told us that if we ever heard a ringing in our ears it was some poor lost soul in purgatory trying to get our attention, trying to get us to say a "Hail Mary" for them, so that they would have some time taken off their sentence in purgatory. At least there was some hope of getting into heaven if we only committed venial sins. But I had somehow or other picked up the idea that mortal sins could not be forgiven. Once someone committed a "mortlar" that was it, they were going to hell and there was no getting out. I really believed this and I must say the thoughts of it terrified me. I wouldn't even go to purgatory now. What was I going to do? – I was going to hell, and I had to make my confirmation soon – Oh God, how was I going to go through with my confirmation?! I had even written to the Archbishop of Dublin, John Charles McQuaid, asking him what his third name was, so that I could take it for my confirmation name, and he had written a personal reply, telling me to take the name Joseph, after Jesus' earthly father.

An intense fear of God came over me. I was terrified of Him. I lay awake many nights thinking about hell and eternity. I would try to get an idea of how long eternity was. I would think of a million years and then a trillion years – would it finish then? No, not even after a million, trillion years . . . I couldn't grasp the length of eternity; I was frightened to even think on it for too long. Nor was I looking forward to my confirmation any more; rather, I was now dreading it.

Chapter Four
Me and the Boys

I'm Dying

Shortly after this episode we began to prepare for Halloween. All the fellas from the Grove used to get together for a few days and collect wood for the bonfire. Ours was usually lit in the middle of the bottom part of the Grove and it was always the biggest bonfire in the north side of Dublin. We were very proud of our bonfire.

On the previous year the corporation workers had come along and taken our wood away from us. Mrs Kennedy had called them and complained that it was dangerous. She was constantly complaining and making trouble for us, sticking her nose in where it wasn't wanted. This year we had a plan. We began collecting wood a little earlier than usual, stashing huge hoards of it in different parts of Gago's land and in St Anne's Estate. Then we gathered another load of it for our *decoy* fire, which we put up a couple of days before Halloween, with the help of some of the bigger boys. We positioned it in the same spot as the previous year's fire, hoping thereby to fool Mrs Kennedy and the corporation. If they removed this fuel, we would still have our hidden stash for the real fire. We were very proud of our amazing plan and of ourselves; neither Mrs Kennedy nor the corporation would stop our fire. Every one of us was sworn to secrecy; nobody dared to say a word to anyone about it. Having set the wood up for the decoy fire in the usual spot for our fire in the park, we lit a smaller fire nearby to keep ourselves warm.

Along with Mrs Kennedy, other people around the Grove were saying that the bonfire was dangerous. Gerry Tracy's ma told us that if one of the rubber spits from the burning car tyres in the bonfire ever hit one of us, it could kill us. She said that it would burn straight through you until it came out the other side. Our imaginations worked overtime. I could picture this burning tar going straight through my heart or neck and killing me very slowly and painfully. We all decided not to go near any burning tyres, because that would be a terrible death.

As it happened, one of the bigger lads threw a car tyre on to the flames as we were standing there. Me and my pals looked at each other and then took a few paces back, just in case the tyre spat at us. Suddenly there was a loud bang and a huge spit of burning rubber shot from the tyre. It came straight at me and hit me just under my right ear on my neck. I let out a terrible scream as I realised the horror of the situation. I was dying and there was nothing I could do about it. I ran as fast as I could to my house, straight to the big green scullery door at the back. The door was locked and I couldn't get in so I screamed as loud as I could, "*Ma, help me, I'm dying!*" I was hysterical. "*The tar is burning a hole through me neck and I'm dying! Oh please, ma, help me!*" My ma came running out and lifted me up in her arms and said in her lovely mother's way, "There now John, sure you're not dying at all – it's only a burn."

"No, ma," I said, "it's rubber off the tyre in the fire and it's going to burn straight through me neck until I'm dead. Mrs Tracy told us." It took all my mother's wisdom and love to calm me down. I stayed in that night and cuddled up beside her for comfort as we watched television together.

I was allowed to stay home from school the following day because of my burn. As expected, the corporation men came at about 11 a.m. and took away the fuel we had set up as a decoy, our pretend fire. Mrs Lounds, our next-door neighbour, was in the house with us at the time and she said, "Oh what a shame, after all the hard work the boys put in to collecting the wood. Mind you," she continued, "they didn't have as much wood this year as what they usually have, did they Alice?"

"I think we're seeing the end of the fires, Mrs Lounds," my

ma replied. "The park committee is getting very strict about this type of thing." I was bursting to tell them about our real fire, and how it was going to be the biggest one yet, but with great difficulty I kept my mouth shut. I had a real sense of victory inside me and it felt good.

Halloween morning came and we all went to school as usual. All the big guys had met the night before and the plan was that everyone would assemble in Gago's at 3 o'clock to get the fire ready for that night. There must have been about 50 of us there at the appointed time. We had ropes, old wheels from prams, home-made trucks – anything that we could use to carry the fuel down to the grove. There was plenty of wood, including huge tree trunks that the big fellows dragged out of Gago's ditch. It took them ages to pull it around to the park. We had all the wood down at the fire-spot by six o'clock; at seven we were ready to light up. The pile of fuel reached over twenty feet high. We didn't put any rubber tyres in it because of what had happened to me, but instead we used petrol. When we lit it the flames shot about 30 feet into the air. Sure enough, it was an awesome sight, the greatest bonfire that Mount Prospect Grove had ever seen. It was also an awesome victory over Mrs Kennedy, the park committee and Dublin Corporation.

My parents were quite pleased at the way we planned the whole operation. It was the talk of the area for a while. Mrs Kennedy and the park committee, however, were furious.

My Confirmation

The weeks passed and nothing had been said to me by anyone about the mirror. My confirmation-day was drawing close and I was getting more nervous about it. My ma and da brought me into town to buy my confirmation clothes. They bought me a lovely dark-grey suit, socks, shoes, shirt, the works. They also bought me a stupid-looking grey hat in Cleary's. The hat had a ridiculous peak and flaps that come over the ears.

"Please, ma, don't buy that hat for me, it's an awful-looking thing."

"Honest, John," my ma said, "it's lovely on you."

"Everyone will laugh at me in this hat," I moaned. It

occurred to me that maybe this was the beginning of my punishment from God for my mortal sin.

Every day at school we learned from the Catechism all the answers to the questions that the bishop might ask. I made sure that I knew them off by heart. He didn't always ask everyone a question, but Mr Cleary had heard "on good authority" that on this occasion the bishop was expected to question each of us. More punishment, I thought. One piece of good news was that John Charles McQuaid would not be the bishop on duty that day. I would have been too "in bits" to speak to him, what with me after committing a mortlar, and then having the cheek to take his name for my confirmation! John Charles McQuaid was close to God because he was the archbishop, so he would probably have been able to tell I had committed a mortlar.

Finally, the great day arrived. My ma helped me dress up in my new suit. I had hidden the awful-looking hat under the stairs, but my sister Geraldine found it.

"I found it, mammy," she said.

"That one's an awful traitor," I thought. I began to plead with my ma, "Aw! Please, ma, don't make me wear it, I hate that hat; it's an awful-looking thing."

"No, John you must wear it, it looks lovely on you and it will look great in the photographs."

St Gabrielle's church was just around the corner from where we lived and so I was allowed to go around on my own in order to meet Kevin and the lads. "I'll see yiz down there, everyone!" I shouted as I left. My entire family were coming to my confirmation. All my sisters were fighting over the bathroom and putting on make-up and doing their hair. My two brothers Eamon and Michael were dressed-up as well. The house was insane that morning; even Rags the dog was running around like a mad thing.

"You go straight down to the church, John," my father said. "We'll meet you at the front door in about twenty minutes."

"And don't get yourself dirty, John," my mam said. She then kissed me and gave me a friendly pat on the behind as I headed off.

"Ok, ma," I answered. The minute that I got out of sight of

the house I took the hat off and stuffed it under my arm so that nobody could see it. When I got to the church the teachers from my school were organising the rest of the lads. Most of them were there already. "Line up in twos," Mr Kennedy shouted at us. We all lined up like little soldiers outside the church. I found Kevin and I lined up beside him.

"What's that under your arm, John?" he said.

"Aw it's j-just Eamon's h-h-hat; I took it by mistake this morning. I'm going to g-give it to him when he comes round to the church l-l-later." Aw no, I thought, I'm lying just before my confirmation. God must really hate me.

"H-how long is this going to take, Kevin?' I asked.

"Dunno," he said. "Probably an hour and a half. Why?"

"'C-Cause I'm b-burstin' to go to the t-toilet."

"Well you can't go now – we're goin' into the chapel."

Then my family appeared beside us. "John Edwards, where is your hat?" my mother asked.

"I'm h-holding it under my arm, ma," I answered. Kevin laughed and said, "You mean to say that awful thing is really your hat?"

"Yeah," I answered. "My m-ma bought it for me, she thinks it's lovely, b-b-but I h-hate it." Kevin couldn't stop laughing. I began to laugh too. He understood. We went all the way down the right-hand side of the church: me, Dennis Purcell and Peter Barry, and we all sat together. There seemed to be hundreds of us making our confirmation. The most important thing to us for the day was how much money we would get from our aunts and uncles. We weren't really interested in the religious side of it and we didn't understand it very well either, even though we had memorised nearly the entire Catechism. The service started when the bishop came in, the choir singing as he walked down the centre aisle of the huge church.

"Janey Mack," I thought, "I'm burstin' to go to the toilet; I hope I can hold on."

The service proceeded until finally the bishop began to ask the questions. It was clear that he intended questioning everyone, just as Mr Cleary had said. I was getting pains in my

side now. "Oh what's keeping him?" I whispered to Peter
Barry. "He's taking so long." I was too afraid to ask the
teachers if I could go out. This was confirmation day and the
bishop was here; I was sure nobody would be allowed out to
the toilet during such an important event. At this stage I was
wriggling in my seat trying to keep it in, and I was crossing my
legs as well. "Would you ever stay still, John!" Kevin said. At
last I could hold on no longer.

A warm feeling came all over my backside and legs as the
urine flowed down and out through the bottom of my short
trousers. My ma would probably kill me, I thought, but I put
my new hat between Peter and me to stop him getting wet. The
urine was dripping off the back of the seat now and everyone
could see it. I sat there trying to pretend that it was someone
else but I was crying inside. This was an awful day – I wished
I could die. I was being punished for breaking the mirror in
Gago's house. I didn't cry, however, but continued looking
straight ahead as if nothing was wrong. I was too afraid to ask
the teachers to let me out.

"What is your name, son?" the bishop asked me.

"J-John Charles," I whispered.

"And what name are you taking for your confirmation,
son?" the Bishop asked.

"Joseph, your grace," I said without stuttering.

"Good. Now can you tell me, what are the seven deadly sins?"

"P-Pride, g-g-gluttony, jealousy . . . " I sweated as we talked,
fearful that my pee would go on the lovely long robe that he
was wearing. He was standing in the middle of a puddle of it
but he didn't seem to notice.

"Good lad," he said as I finished naming the seven deadliers.
Then he blessed me and moved on to Peter Barry.

When the service finished we all walked out in twos again.
I was still holding on to my bladder, so as soon as I got out I
ran around the back of the church and had a lovely, long pee
against the wall. I was grateful that the suit's dark grey colour
camouflaged the wet mark very well. Quickly I returned to the
front of the church and posed with the others for all the
photographs. Nobody said a word to me about my wetting

myself during the service. I took a swift look at the bishop on the way out and he didn't have any wet marks on his robe.

We went home for a family dinner before having more photographs taken by Peter Barry's da up at number five. He worked for the *Irish Times* – in fact he was personal photographer for President Eamon De Valera, so we were going to have the best photographs of the whole school and they might even get printed in the newspaper.

"Did the bishop ask you a question, John?" Maeve asked me.

"Yeah," I said.

"Well – what was it?" Pauline asked.

"He w-wanted to know what the seven d-deadly s-sins were."

"Why? Didn't he know himself?" my dad joked.

"HAW! HAW!" we all shouted sarcastically. I was still wearing my wet shorts and they were beginning to rub painfully against the top of my legs. Luckily the hat only got a tiny bit wet and I was able to wear it for the photographs after church.

As my mother brushed my hair for me before we went up to Barry's house for the photographs, she gently patted my behind, as if to confirm what she had suspected.

"Right, young man, you're ready for the photos," she said. I looked up at her and I could see in her eyes that she knew I had wet my trousers. She had a look of such love in them, mixed with pain for me. I held my breath and tried to think of some excuse to explain why my pants were wet. Then she said, "You must have sat on something wet, John. Now go on and have your photos done and we will dry your pants when you get back." I loved my ma; she was so understanding. When I came back later she had the immersion heater on, and the water was extremely hot. She gave my pants a quick wash and put them on the hot boiler. They were dry, ironed, and as good as new before long.

Later we went to visit all my uncles and aunts. I got about seven pounds from them. I was loaded. Neither Peter Barry nor Kevin ever said a word to me about my miserable experience on my confirmation day.

Chapter Five
More About My Ma and Da

Robbing Orchards

My mother was a great cook; she was always baking cakes and pies and scones and bread and all that sort of thing. We would often come in from school to find home-made brown and white bread wrapped in tea towels and sitting on the windowsill of the kitchen, the mouth-watering aroma filling the entire room. One of our favourites was her apple tart. Often we would plead with her, "Ma, make some apple tart today, will ye?"

"I can't, because I have no apples – not unless you get me some," she would say. My ma didn't have many faults but this was one area where she was too lenient with us, even encouraging us in our mischief. "Mrs Hurding down in number 20 has lovely apples on her tree at the moment; so has Mrs Kennedy around the corner. Go and get some for us, will you – but don't get caught."

Geraldine and I would put on our orchard-robbing jumpers and prepare to get some apples for my ma. It was like setting off on an exciting mission. "We won't be long, ma!" we shouted as we left the house.

"I only need a few now so don't bring back a lot," she called after us. We didn't pay attention to that, however; we reckoned that the more we brought back the more pleased she would be and also the more apple tarts she would make. Off we ran down the lane behind our house, stopping to peep over Mrs Hurding's wall. Once we were sure the coast was clear Geraldine and I would tuck the ends of our jumpers into our trousers and jump over the wall. Then crouching as low as we could, we would run across the garden to the cooking-apple trees.

First we would grab any apples that had fallen on the ground but were in good condition. Then we picked as many as we could reach on the trees and stuffed them down our jumpers, all the time watching to see if anyone were coming. Finally, like soldiers who had completed a successful mission, we would return home to a hero's welcome from our mother.

"Here you are, ma," we'd say, placing maybe 50 or 60 apples on the kitchen table for her.

"Oh merciful heaven, what are you doing bringing me home so many apples? I only wanted a few, not the whole orchard! – Did anyone see you?"

"No, ma," we'd say with pride. "Nobody saw us at all."

"Good then, but don't tell your father!"

"Don't worry about that ma," we'd reply; nor were we likely to tell him. What he didn't know wouldn't hurt him – or us.

A Glimpse of the Snake Pit

There was trouble brewing in McCairns' Motors, the company my father worked for. Jerry Jordison and Noel Brooks were two of the men who were in management with him. They were university-educated men, unlike my father, and I used to think they were jealous of him. I hated when they came to our home because I could sense the struggle between them. They would come in and put a load of papers on the table and talk for ages about them. My da was upset sometimes when they left. He was drinking more than ever, and because he was at this time working at home instead of on the company premises, he was able to drink while he worked. He used the living room as his office, and as he was often sick while he was working he would place an old newspaper on the floor with a red basin on top of it. He hardly ate at all, but just worked and drank at the same time, getting sick every so often and spitting horrible green phlegm into the basin. Sometimes he sent me on my bike to the Dollymount Inn to get drink for him. The atmosphere in the house during those times was terrible. Da got extremely cranky and fussy, and my sister Pauline left home and went to live in

Portugal because he was being so strict with her. He wouldn't allow her to wear trouser suits, stay out late at the weekends, or wear the make-up she liked.

One day when I came home from school an ambulance was standing outside our house. My da was being taken into hospital. I hated ambulances; they always spoke of death to me.

"Mammy, is daddy dying?" I asked her.

"No, son," she said. "He is just going in for a rest."

At the hospital they discovered that he had malnutrition from not eating and ulcers from all the drink he had taken. Evelyn, Maeve and my ma were allowed to see him. He was very sick, they said; I was afraid that he was going to die.

One morning after breakfast I walked out into the hallway of our house to find my mam holding my father's Trilby hat and crying. There were great big tears rolling down her cheeks.

'W-w-what's wrong m-mammy, is daddy all r-right?"

"Daddy might never come home again," my mam said, and she broke down weeping. I had never seen her like this before. I didn't know what to do so I gave her a big hug. She hung on to me for ages and just cried and cried.

My sister Pauline had settled in Portugal by now and she had found a job as an English teacher. I thought she was very brave to go away so far. Her ex-boyfriend Dermot was like one of the family and he kept coming around to see us. I loved Dermot; he was so good to me and spent loads of time with me. Every Sunday he brought me to his ma's house in Eastwall, down near the docks, for a delicious Sunday dinner. The whole family sat out in a little room with a glass roof and ate huge dinners: lamb or chicken or pork with loads of mashed spuds and mushy peas (my favourite) smothered with gravy. They all loved me, and if I couldn't make it on any Sunday they would be very upset, especially Dermot's ma. Next to my Auntie Eileen, Mrs Lynch came closest to being like a granny to me. I felt really welcome there and I felt special. There wasn't a whole gang of brothers and sisters to compete with.

One summer's day Dermot brought me to see my father in hospital. He had been moved from the Mater hospital in North Dublin to St John of God's hospital in Stillorgan, which is on the south side of the city. This was a hospital for people with alcohol and drug problems and, my mother told me, it was very expensive to stay in. Dermot carried me on his big blue Heinkel motor scooter. The hospital was a lovely place: "Like a five-star hotel," Dermot said; I took his word for it because I had never stayed in a five-star hotel. It was a beautifully sunny day, with hardly a cloud in the sky. As we approached the hospital gates I could see the long driveway with lovely trees lining both sides. Beyond the trees on one side there was a handball alley, and on the other there was a big garden where some people were playing croquet. In the distance I could see Howth Head and Clontarf. I thought that if I had binoculars I would be able to spot our house.

My heart pounded as we passed through the big front doors into the reception area. I was about to see my father again. I had never seen him in hospital before; I always thought that he was too strong and wise to end up in hospital.

"Could you tell us which room Mr Edwards is in, please?" Dermot asked the nurse at the desk. "Mr *Eddie* Edwards," he added. The receptionist checked the register and then she said, "I am afraid that you cannot see Mr Edwards today. He has taken a turn for the worse and is asleep at the moment."

"Can we just go up to see him for a minute?" Dermot pleaded. "This is John, Mr Edwards' son and he has not seen him in a couple of weeks. He has a card and some King Edward cigars to give to his dad."

"I am sorry, Mr Lynch, but the boy cannot go in to see him today. He will be allowed see him in a few day's time. You may leave the presents by his bed if you like, Mr Lynch, but the boy must wait here."

"Thanks – I will," Dermot said. "John, you wait here till I come back. I promise you I won't be long."

"P-put the card beside his bed where he can see it, Dermot, will you?"

"'Course I will, John, I'll put it in a spot where he can't miss it, OK?"

I sat in a big chair in the reception area while I waited for Dermot. I was worried about my da. What could be wrong with him? Why wouldn't they let me see him? So many questions were going around in my head. As I sat there a number of people walked past me in their dressing gowns and slippers, and I wondered if they were all alcoholics like my father. The atmosphere was pleasant, however, and the people were friendly. I remember being surprised by the number of priests and nuns working in the place. It was only afterwards that I discovered that the nuns and priests were patients there too.

After about ten minutes, Dermot returned.

"John," he said, "your da's fine. He is asleep but he is fine. I will bring you back to see him next week when he is a bit better." I was very relieved to hear this. My biggest fear was that he would die and leave me. I loved my da so much. He was still the best da in the world as far as I was concerned.

As we left the building I asked Dermot to show me which room my da was in.

"He is up in that room there, John," he said, pointing to a small window above our heads. I was shocked to see that it had iron bars on it. I could not believe that my da, the best da in the world, was in a room behind bars. He was still my hero in many ways, despite his drinking and his strictness, and I was so proud of him, no matter what he did. I wished that this moment would go away because I couldn't come to terms with it. *My da was in a room with bars on the window . . .*

"Dermot, why are there bars on the window?"

"The drink made him a bit sick, John," he said. "The doctors need to keep him in there for a couple of days. It's a special room for people who are sick with the drink." I learned later that they called this room the snake pit, because of the hallucinations the patients had while they dried out.

I held on to Dermot all the way home on the Heinkel. Tears streamed from my eyes as I thought of my da in the room with the bars on it – and they weren't caused by the wind on my face.

Chapter Six
Times They Are A-Changing

Secondary School

I was now about twelve years old. I was struggling within myself, trying desperately to come to terms with the turmoil I was feeling. Puberty had arrived, my body was changing, I was beginning to fancy girls; but because of my stutter I could not talk to them the way I wanted to. I really put myself down for this.

I had also at this time to face an examination for acceptance in St Paul's Secondary School. Most of my pals were going to St Paul's and it was very important for me to pass this exam. Kevin Purcell, my best friend, was heading off to boarding school. With all that was going on in my life at the time I found it impossible to concentrate during the exam. The results arrived a couple of weeks later and my heart broke as I read the words:

We are sorry to inform you that you have not managed to pass the entrance exam to St Paul's school. Therefore you have failed to secure a place in the school. We do however wish you every success for your future.

I stood in the sitting room of our house holding on to the letter of rejection. I had failed, and I didn't know what to do. How would I tell my da? He would think I was such a failure. What school would I go to? All my friends will have passed the exam and I will be the only one who has failed! I knew this was the way it would be. I would have to make new friends and maybe they would laugh at my stutter.

Something died in me that day. I lost the will to fight for myself. I didn't see how I could cope any more. I cried and cried as I looked out of the window. The park didn't seem the same somehow. Life was taking on a different meaning; it was getting more serious, far too serious, and I didn't like it. The corporation had cut the elm trees down during that summer. The mailer tree, the hut, the swing, it was all gone. They were building flats in Gago's field and Kevin was going to boarding school, and I had failed to get into St Paul's *and* my da was in hospital. Mammy said that he was an alcoholic – I didn't believe that, however.

One day I went to see him, and he was looking very well, eating again, putting weight on, and even telling jokes. We had a game of croquet out on the lawn. It was a good day, and for a few hours we were happy. I gave him a box of King Edward cigars; he wrestled me for them and rubbed me on my face with his stubbly chin. He wore a great big smile all that day. I managed to tell him about failing the St Paul's entrance exam. He told me that I shouldn't worry; I was sure to find a better school. I cried myself to sleep that night.

Six weeks later he left the hospital. He was looking great and he was fun to be with. He and my ma were going to Portugal for a holiday and, of course, to visit my sister Pauline. They were bringing Geraldine with them. I was a bit jealous of this; Geraldine was only eighteen months older than me and she was very excited about going. I didn't say a word about how I felt, however, because my da said that when they came home we were all going to take another holiday in Bangor in Northern Ireland. There was something secretive about the preparations for the Portuguese trip. Nobody talked about it in front of me, and I wondered if Pauline was pregnant. As I listened in on some conversations and noticed one or two bits of baby clothes around the house I put one and one together. I couldn't understand why they didn't just tell me. I always seemed to know a lot more than everyone realised. I had learned to read people and situations very well, sometimes too well.

TIMES THEY ARE A-CHANGING

One night about a week before they were due to leave my parents called me into the living room.

"John," my father said, with obvious delight, "you're coming with us to Portugal."

"Janey Mack, da, that's f-fantastic!" I said as I hugged them both. "Oh! Wow, can I tell my friends?"

"Yes you can," my dad said. He was enjoying my delight at the news. Within half an hour I had called to see nearly all of my friends. I might not have got into St Paul's school but I was going to Portugal! I felt reinstated as far as the success stakes were concerned.

The night before our departure we packed and put everything into my mother's brand-new red Simca 1000 car that my dad had bought her for her birthday. I could hardly sleep that night I was so excited; life wasn't too bad after all.

The St Patrick ferry was a huge, white ship and it must have carried about 200 cars. It was very windy when we arrived and I can remember my mother saying she hoped she didn't get seasick. This will be a great holiday, I thought. As soon as we embarked we settled in a quiet corner of the lounge bar. We could relax there, my da said, and us kids could sleep if we wanted to. After all, the journey would take us 22 hours. I noticed a look of concern on my mother's face as she said, "Eddie, are you sure it's a good idea to stay in the bar?"

"I'll be fine Alice, don't you worry," he responded.

As soon as the boat got under way I went off to investigate every corner of every deck. After about an hour I returned and discovered my mother sitting there looking very upset. My da had a pint of Guinness in front of him and Geraldine had gone off somewhere. In spite of her feelings my ma handled the situation very well because she had seen my da going back on the drink so many times before. I was used to it now as well but each time he did it my heart sank.

When Geraldine came back my ma called both of us to her side. "I want to talk to you, John," she said. I could see by Geraldine's face that she already knew what my ma wanted to talk about. She had that look of being one up on me. My ma took some photographs from her handbag, and carefully placing them in my hands she said, "John, this is Pilar, Pauline's baby. You're an uncle, John." I was a bit embarrassed, but I replied simply, "I was w-wondering when you were going to tell me. I've known for ages, ma. I'm not s-stupid, you know."

My ma was taken completely by surprise. She had some long explanation ready to give me but now she didn't know what to say. "It's a lovely baby," I said. "Who's the da?"

"Caesar is his name, Caesar Augusto de Medina Ferro."

"What?" I said, laughing hysterically. "Caesar Augustus! My sister is going out with Caesar Augustus! Oh ma, that's gas." We all had a laugh about it and this helped to relieve the tension of the situation.

My da drank all the way through the holiday. One night he was so tired and drunk he left the luggage on the roof rack while we slept. When we got up the next morning it was gone. My ma was very upset. Everything we brought with us had been taken. I was cursing the drink. We went to an open-air bar to try to decide what to do. My father ordered "Quatro bier, por favor."

"No, no," the waiter said, assuming that two of the beers were for Geraldine and me.

"*Dos* for him and *dos* for me," said my ma, indicating my da and herself.

The local police managed to recover the bags for us that afternoon. Thankfully there were only a few things missing. We drove over the Pyrenees Mountains and on down to Lisbon. Pauline was excited to see us, and my ma and da were like two young things when they saw the baby. My ma, Pauline and Geraldine chattered on about the usual things regarding babies.

"How was the birth, Pauline? Oh you poor thing!" my ma added, as Pauline told her about the stitches. "Do you know, your next baby will be easy; I had Evelyn after you, Pauline, and she came out of me like a cork out of a bottle. I hardly even knew that I had her, an' she was over seven pounds."

"They're off," I said to my father, as the two of us walked out onto the balcony of Pauline's apartment. "Caesar Augustus is c-coming around tonight, da. I wonder if he w-wears one of those long robes and them f-flowers on his head," I joked.

"I hope not," my da said, laughing.

Caesar arrived that night and he was a nice, quiet guy, speaking in broken English. My parents both liked him and that was all that really mattered.

We had two glorious weeks in Portugal with Pauline, Caesar and my new niece, Pilar. This was my first trip abroad. When I returned years later my purpose would be very different: to try and kick my drug habit.

Soon after our return to Ireland we headed off on another holiday, this time to Mrs Greenfield's Bed-and-Breakfast in Bangor, Northern Ireland. We drove through Belfast on July the twelfth. The Orange marches were in full swing as we passed through the city. Crowds of onlookers cheered the marchers on, waving Union Jack flags. The troubles had not yet broken out and everyone seemed to be just having a great time. Within a few short years the Twelfth of July marches would take on a completely different meaning for many.

We had a good time up in Mrs Greenfield's. Uncle Jimmy and Auntie Joan were with us. They weren't really related but were close friends of the family. Every night Uncle Jimmy, Auntie Joan and my parents would go out to the pub. My dad's drinking was getting bad again, and he had reverted to his old habit of bringing a few bottles home with him when the pub closed. I was desperate to please him and make him happy. Some days I would hire a rowing boat and go out fishing. I would row out to just beyond the little harbour in Bangor and then I would let my hand-line, with my shiny silver spinner, hang out from the back of the boat. I desperately wanted to catch a fish, not so much for myself but to try and please my da. I only caught one fish out of about five fishing trips in the little boat, but because of my determination to get my dad's attention and impress him I would buy five or six mackerel from the fishermen I met on my way back and pretend to my dad that I had caught them.

"Look what I caught, da," I'd say. I would fill up with joy when he responded to me with a big "Well done son."

"Look at the size of this one," I'd continue, holding up the biggest of the mackerel.

"Wow! We'll have to get Mrs Greenfield to cook that one for us tonight."

"Don't you ever catch anything besides mackerel out there?" my Uncle Jimmy asked me one day. "I fancy a bit of codling or haddock."

I felt embarrassed, and guilty. "There only seems to be mackerel," I said, my face red.

I began to notice some changes to my body while I was up in Bangor; my voice too was changing. It was beginning to break, and to my horror it would croak or squeak sometimes as I temporarily lost control of my voice level. Everyone thought this was hilarious.

"John's voice is breaking," Geraldine teased. "You sound like a broken foghorn." With that everyone would be in an uproar. I hated when people jeered at me like that. I would run out of the room and hide upstairs. Why can't they see I am a sensitive person, I would ask myself. Don't they know that they are hurting me, hurting me deeply? I would allow myself feel the pain for a moment and then push it down somewhere inside myself.

When we arrived home in Dublin at the end of July there was a letter waiting, informing me that I had been accepted in the De La Salle School in Donaghmede. This was about three miles from our house and I could easily cycle to it. It was a new school and I was one of the first pupils. I was very relieved to have been accepted somewhere – anywhere – not so much because I wanted to be a great scholar but because I would no longer be the odd one out among my friends.

I called down to Kevin's' house to tell him the good news and he was pleased for me. We could both sense that life was changing fast; in a couple of weeks he was going off to boarding school. He was experiencing puberty as well and his voice was croaking, like my own. We laughed about our voices – we were pals, after all, so that made it okay. The rest of the Jinx gang were all starting in different schools, with the exception of Peter Barry and David McDermot, who would be with me in De La Salle.

TIMES THEY ARE A-CHANGING

Our Last Days Together

The Jinx gang was about to break up and we all knew it. There were just a few weeks left before our summer holidays were due to end, so we were eager to make the most of the time. Almost every day we went up to St Anne's Estate on our bikes, scrambling over the hills near the old lake, whooping and laughing as we cycled at speed over the top of the small slopes. Sometimes we laid our bikes on the ground and chased each other, frolicking about like young goats.

"This is my hill," I cried, as I ran to some tiny summit.

"Oh no, it's not!" Kevin or Ritchie, Paddy, Peter or little Kevin responded, and we fought each other to try to capture the hill from one another. The victor would then stand on top and say, "I am the champion!"

"Oh no you're not!" and so the battle continued, for what seemed like hours, until we all collapsed in an exhausted heap. Then we set off home, ravenous with hunger and ready for our tea.

"I'm off out again, ma!" Tea was over and I was away with the lads. Sometimes in the evening we held races around the Grove. (Our dads had reckoned that four times around the Grove was a mile.) I always enjoyed this. I was a very good runner and seldom if ever got beaten. I felt free when I ran, like I was in charge and out on my own, a confidence welling up in me that nothing could touch. I wanted to be a professional runner and maybe run for Ireland one day. I believed I was good enough. When we finished our races we would sit in the park and just talk amongst ourselves, remaining there until going home time. "Coming, ma!" we each of us shouted as our respective mams called us in for the night.

Those days seemed to go by very quickly, but they will always remain in my memory. It was no time at all until Kevin had to go away to boarding school. We spent that last day in his house, his mam packing and fussing over him. "Remember to keep yourself clean and wash behind your ears. I wish you were as clean as John Edwards." (This was a comparison I often heard her make.) "Look, Kevin, I have put your name on everything so you don't lose anything, OK?

And you have enough underpants to dress an army so don't forget to change them."

"Yes ma," was his patient reply. I think that Kevin was eventually glad to get out of the door and into the car. I can remember clearly standing on the footpath outside his house as the realisation came over me stronger than ever that life was never going to be the same again. I watched the car drive away and gave Kevin one final wave as it left the Grove.

The Day My Life Changed

I started in my new school that same week, and as Peter Barry and I cycled in on the first day we were both nervous, sensing that secondary school signalled the end of one period in our lives and the beginning of another. We took our time going through St Anne's Estate, trying to psyche ourselves up before actually arriving. The closer we got to Donaghmede the more boys we saw, some cycling and others walking towards the new school. Donaghmede Estate was a new development; hundreds of new houses were being built around the area, and the new school was a part of this development. The road vanished under a layer of mud for the last half-mile before reaching the school, and the mud sprayed up from our front wheels onto our new trousers, making a mess of them.

"Oh no," I thought, "me ma will go nuts when she sees the dirt on these trousers."

The school itself was not much better. It consisted of a big prefabricated hut with three classes and an office. Brother Cadgiton was standing at the front of the building waiting to meet us. He was a big man with a mop of wavy white hair, and he was dressed in a long flowing black robe with two little wings sticking out of the collar at the neck. "Oh well, Peter, here goes," I said as we cycled through the mud up to the entrance.

I must say secondary school was better than I expected. I made friends fairly quickly with some of the other students. John Banahan, or Beano, as we soon re-named him, sat beside me. He was an expert on motorbikes, or so he thought. Then there was Kenneth Fogarty, who was one of the clowns of the class and a very likeable sort of fellow. Brian Duff was another good guy to hang out with. He was the politician of the school, being something of a socialist, if I remember correctly.

My stutter was not as much of a stumbling block to me in secondary school as it had been before. The teachers were sensitive about it most of the time, and the lads here were more mature than my former schoolmates and showed me more respect. A boy called Aidan Brown did try to bully me. I decided to bide my time and sort him out when the occasion arose. I didn't have to wait long. One day just two weeks after school began we were out in the backfield and Aidan, who was sitting up on the high branches of a tree, began shouting down names at me.

"Edwards you're a stupid eejit!"

"Is that right, Browner?" I replied. "Well, see how stupid this is." With that I picked up several large stones from the side of the field.

"Don't you dare throw them at me," he shouted. "If you do I'll kill you."

I didn't pay any attention to his threat but taking careful aim I began to fire the big stones at him. One of them hit him on the side of the head, rattling him so much that he almost fell out of the tree. I threw another couple at him, and at this stage all the boys in the field were watching. As soon as he climbed down to ground level I walked right up to him and socked him in the jaw as hard as I could. He was much bigger than me and I was sure that he could beat me in a fair fight – but who was fighting fair?

"Say you're s-sorry for calling me an eejit," I demanded. He hesitated and I raised my fist to hit him again, when to my relief he said, "I'm sorry."

"What's that?" I said. "I c-can't hear you." I wanted the other boys in the field to hear him as well.

"I'm sorry," he repeated, this time in a louder voice. I was satisfied that everyone had heard him, so I said "Right – let's shake on it . . . " and I held out my hand to him.

"OK," he said, and that was the end of that. I believed in standing up for myself, although this would unfortunately lead me into trouble later on with one of the teachers.

WALKING FREE

Science was my favourite school subject. One day the science teacher Mr Conners was showing us how sulphur burns when you put it in water. He was standing at the front of the class, with his desk raised about eighteen inches so that everyone could see properly as he taught us. "Here you have sulphur," he began. "If you put it in water it burns . . . " and as he was speaking he broke a bit of the sulphur and held it in his hand. As he continued to speak he obviously intended to put the small piece in the water, but for some reason he got confused and put the bigger piece in instead. A look of horror came over his face as he realised what he had done. We could see the lump of sulphur fizzing in the bowl. It looked like it was going to explode.

"Quickly, everyone, down on the floor, and under your desks!" he shouted hysterically. "MOVE!" He was panic-stricken. We all dived for cover and had hardly hit the floor when there was a whooshing noise as the sulphur exploded, destroying Mr Conners' desk and damaging the ceiling over it. Otherwise there was no great harm done. We all thought it was great fun and wished exciting things like that would happen more often in school.

I didn't have many friends in my own neighbourhood at this time, with Kevin away and the other members of the Jinx gang all going their separate ways. I didn't seem to have much in common with them any more. During the summer holidays we all met up again and tried to make a go of our friendships, but Kevin spent most of his time visiting his new schoolfriends, and the other lads were just not around as much. I began to look about for other people to hang out with. Dublin Corporation were building a new community centre down beside St Gabriel's church and a number of young people used to hang around there. There were about twenty of them all together, including several girls, one of whom I fancied.

One summer day Kevin, a few members of the old gang and myself walked past the community centre. As usual the new crowd of young people were hanging about outside it. I quite clearly remember saying to the lads, "I'm going over to get to know these people. See you later." With that I walked away from my childhood buddies. That decision was to change the whole course of my life.

I very quickly got to know the other gang members and became very close to three brothers, Danny, Ron and Eddie Fitzgerald. I also proved to be quite popular with the ladies.

"This is the life," I thought, "having fun and going out with girls."

Yet deep down I was very frightened. I was totally insecure and depressed. My dad's drinking had increased to the point where he was making his own home-brewed wine and beer. He would drink it as soon as or even before it was mature. He was himself greatly depressed and was still working entirely from home because he was too sick to go to the office. I lost interest in my schoolwork and stopped putting any effort into my studies. I was under a lot of pressure and I was looking for a way out. My mother was on Valium anti-depression tablets because of the strain she was under and they seemed to help her come to terms with her lot in life. The atmosphere in the house was absolutely miserable at this time and quite frankly I didn't know how to cope with it any longer.

One day, while I was still only about thirteen, I went to my mother's handbag when she was out of the room. I knew that she kept her Valium in a bottle in the bag. I took the bottle out and, quickly unscrewing the top, I slipped a tablet out of it into my pocket. Then I carefully put the bottle back in its place in my ma's bag.

I waited until after we had had our tea and then went up to my room. I sat down on the end of my bed and took the yellow tablet out of my pocket. I examined it carefully. It had *Roche* imprinted on one side of it and *5mg* on the other. How can one tablet this small help me, I wondered. I knew that I was depressed and needed help but could this one little tablet hold the answer to my problems? Well, there's only one way to find out, I thought, and putting the pill on the end of my tongue I drew it into my mouth. It tasted a little bit sweet but quite unpleasant. I then chewed and swallowed it and drank some cold water from the bathroom to wash the taste away.

WALKING FREE

Five minutes passed and there was no effect; after ten minutes there was still nothing. After fifteen minutes, just when I began to think that I had wasted my time, a sense of calm began to steal over me. A feeling of wellbeing slowly flooded my mind and the knot in my tummy began to loosen. I sat down again on the end of my bed and breathed a great sigh of relief. I had at last found something to help me and give me some rest from my inner turmoil.

I came downstairs and watched telly for a while. My dad was in the room and he was getting sick into a bowl that was standing on an old newspaper in front of him on the floor. Funny, it didn't seem to bother me too much that night. I slept very well and when I awoke the next morning I was still feeling good. School was easier to handle as well. I remember thinking during that day that those Valium were great. I continued to steal them from my ma's handbag and after a couple of weeks I needed two at a time to get the same effect – and sometimes three.

I began to skip my homework and go out with the lads at night. Danny was sixteen and both he and another new friend Jimmy Bruen were working. They had enough money to buy cider sometimes and drink it up in the woods. We were eventually to name this woods "Johnny's Woods", after me. I began to drink cider with the lads. I discovered that if I drank cider on top of the Valium it had a greater effect. We also began to smoke hash, which was quite cheap in those days at about eleven pounds an ounce. We would chip in our money and buy several pound deals.

This was 1967; the drug scene was just beginning to hit Ireland; hippies were all the rage and Scott Mackenzie was singing a song about going to San Francisco and having flowers in your hair.

Our gang began to mix with an older bunch of lads from our neighbourhood. They were taking harder drugs, even injecting. They could be seen falling about the place, stoned out of their minds, down by the seafront at Dollymount. We all thought that they were very foolish to inject and we promised ourselves that we would never do that. We were in control and we would keep it that way. Yet somehow we looked up to these guys; they were different and as far as we were concerned it was cool to get stoned.

I was getting a bit of a reputation in my neighbourhood and amongst my peers as a drug user. In school many of the lads looked up to me because of this reputation. I still looked at myself through other people's eyes and therefore I felt good about this new-found respect. Sometimes I would bring in hash to school and show it to the lads. On one occasion I made up a mixture from turf and an Oxo cube and convinced some of my schoolmates that it was hash. They thought that I was cool. I began to let my hair grow and I smoked cigarettes every day. I cycled an old Velo Solex bike. This was a big, black, heavy bike with a footrest in the "v" of the frame. There had originally been an engine on the front wheel for driving, but I had removed this because I wasn't old enough to have a motorbike yet. I dressed in wide bellbottoms and always wore a big old black army coat that reached down to below my knees. My particular trademark was an old brown Trilby hat pulled down at just the right angle over my right eye. I thought that I was the bees' knees.

One day in January of 1969 I was at school as usual, and our first class after lunch was history with Mr Finneran teaching. He was a hard teacher and corporal punishment was one of the tools he used to keep order in the class. I had moved back to sit beside Ken Fogarty that day because the boy who normally sat beside me was absent.

"Right, everyone, get out your history books," Mr Finneran commanded. I fumbled for mine in my bag and couldn't find it. I had unfortunately left it under the desk without realising it.

"Edwards!" Mr Finneran shouted. "Get your history book out, now."

"I c-can't find it, sir," I said. I was still looking in my bag when Mr Finneran came charging towards me. He grabbed my bag from me and emptied out the contents on top of my desk.

"Where is your book?" he roared and he began to hit me full force with his fists around my head. I felt humiliated in front of the class, and he was really hurting me.

"Stop it!" I shouted. He laughed at me when I said that and continued to hit me. Some of the other boys in the class began to laugh also. I then lost my temper and hit out at Mr Finneran, punching him several times. He backed off and said, "You've done it this time, Edwards." He promptly left the room and returned with Brother Cadgiton, the headmaster.

"Come out to the office, Edwards," the head said. I got a severe telling-off for hitting the teacher and was told that I would probably be expelled. With that I was sent home.

I tried to explain to my dad what had happened but he was furious with me for apparently creating this problem in the classroom.

"It wasn't my fault, da," I said. "Finneran was h-hitting me real hard, I had to d-do something to defend myself." My father was not convinced. On the following day he came with me to the school. Brother Cadgiton took him into his office to speak to him and I was left sitting out in the car. I was in turmoil as I sat there. On the one hand I would have liked to remain in school, but there was also a big part of me that wanted to get a job and have some money to spend for a change. I was angry with all the teachers, feeling sure that not one of them would stand up for me. I may have been a bad pupil, I was certainly taking some drugs and drinking, but Mr Finneran had been in the wrong this time. He had given me an awful beating. I was frustrated also because I couldn't stand up for myself.

After what seemed like an hour my da came out of Cadgiton's office. I searched his face for signs of anger. There were none but instead he had a look of defeat about him. He appeared sad and I felt horrible, like I had let him down. I was screaming inside, "This is not my fault" "This is not my fault". I couldn't say it to my dad because I felt he wouldn't hear me if I did. Once again he was bitterly disappointed in me. I felt such a failure. Strangely enough, all I wanted at that moment was for him to give me a hug and reassure me that everything was going to be okay.

"That is your schooling finished, John," my da said, "and you're not even sixteen yet." That was all he said. He kept quiet the rest of the way home and the silence was deafening.

TIMES THEY ARE A-CHANGING

I was four months away from my intermediate exams, had no qualifications and was taking drugs and drinking too much. I was frightened of what the future held for me.

Chapter Seven
My First Job
and My Last Bomb

My da wasted no time at all. The next day was a Saturday. He called me up to his bedroom for a chat. I hated those chats with my da; they were more like lectures and they could go on for several hours. He was sitting up in his bed, a cup of hot tea beside him and newspapers spread all round him.

"I have been looking for some jobs for you, John. I have pinpointed two that I believe you could start fairly quickly." I began to comment but he cut me off and continued, "One job is as a silk-screen printer with Danny Fitzgerald's father; he has vacancies at the moment and is willing to give you a start. The other is in hairdressing. Your sister Evelyn is willing to give you a job in her salon if you are prepared to get training in a top Dublin salon. Which do you want to do, John?"

I felt very much like I was being put on the spot. I was not expecting my da to have this kind of a chat with me. I knew my future was at stake here. On the one hand this was an important decision I had to make; on the other hand I couldn't have cared less. My attitude was one of "Who cares?" Since I had begun to smoke hash I had lost any sense of ambition or desire to better myself. For a brief moment the importance of this conversation and its consequences struck me. Then I shrugged my shoulders and said I chose hairdressing.

My father applied for a job for me at Lionell's of Wicklow Street, one of the top hairdressing salons in Dublin at the time. I was asked to come in for an interview the following week. On the day of the interview I was really nervous. Lionel himself talked with me and made me feel at ease. After half-an-hour he said, "Can you start next Monday?"

"O-of course I c-can," I stuttered.

I was now earning money – not much, mind you – but the tips were good. I got enough on tips to live on. We received 10% commission for selling conditioner to the women coming into the shop. Every woman whose hair I washed got conditioner, whether she wanted it or not. I earned enough from this to go out on Saturday nights with the boys. I gave my mother a few quid a week to keep her happy; the rest I could spend on myself.

My new mates Danny, Eddie and Ron, along with Jimmy Bruen, began to call round for me during the week. We would buy a few bottles of cider and some hash and go up to St Anne's park or down the seafront near the Dollymount Inn. We had begun to get involved in a very dangerous hobby: bomb-making. We were never involved in the political troubles in Ireland – in fact we didn't understand much about any of that – but when we were younger we had seen some of the older lads make what they called copper bombs. We had learned how to make these and now for a season we began to have what we thought was a "bit of crack" with them. The Dublin newspapers often carried stories about boys blowing their hands off while making these bombs and some had even been killed. They were deadly. We would make a few of these and bring them up to St Anne's Estate to let them off and have a bit of fun.

At St Anne's we would first enjoy a few bottles of cider and a smoke of dope. When we were sufficiently stoned we dug a hole at the base of one of the big Gaelic football posts and put a pipe bomb in the hole. Fuses of equal length and width would then be placed. These fuses were long enough to give us time to get away without being blown up. Then at exactly the same time we each lit a fuse and ran like mad, diving for cover behind the trees next to the posts. Ten or fifteen heads would then peep out to see how high the goalposts would go up in the air. This was the point of the whole exercise.

The seconds passed, and tingling all over with excitement we waited to hear a couple of mighty explosions – BANG!

MY FIRST JOB AND MY LAST BOMB

BANG! *"Yeeaah!"* we would shout, as the goalposts were launched several feet into the air.

Some of the older guys that we had begun to hang around with had taken this pipe-bomb making to another level. We sometimes went with them at night to rob bus stops. They were made of steel and were about ten feet long and a quarter inch thick. Sometimes we stole large red fire extinguishers instead. With these materials and the aid of a sledgehammer we made bigger and more deadly bombs. One night the gang went up to St Anne's park. The plan was to have a good booze-up and smoke and then let a big bomb off.

The park used to be owned by the Guinness family. There was a mile-long road that led up to where the mansion was, and at the beginning of this driveway there was a small concrete hut. This hut housed the electricity link for the estate from the Electricity Supply Board. The hut had walls over a foot thick and an iron door on the front of it. Everyone got fairly stoned and drunk. The evening was spent partying and getting psyched-up for the blast. The older lads had brought a big red fire extinguisher with them and it was filled to capacity with explosives. A hole was dug in the ground at the base of the electricity hut and the bomb was placed in it. This one had an extra-long fuse, which someone eventually lit. Everyone agreed to wait long enough to see how big the hole in the wall was before leaving the park; then we would split and meet again later on. The fuse hissed as it burnt and the flame slowly crept towards the bomb. Everyone ran as fast as they could and hid behind the big pine trees that surrounded the hut.

"Cover your ears," someone shouted, "this is going to be a big one!"

Suddenly there was a huge explosion, and the earth actually shook beneath us. This was by far the biggest bomb that any of us had ever been involved with. We didn't think it would be so loud. Next thing I knew bricks, mortar and dust rained down on the gang through the trees. Everyone was stunned. The dust began to settle and we tried to pull ourselves together. The blast had dulled our hearing, leaving the sensation of having cotton wool in our ears. We ventured back to where the hut had been.

We expected to see a big hole in the side of it, but instead there was nothing. The hut had been shattered to smithereens. The iron door had been blown across the road and lay mangled on the football pitch. Everyone appeared shocked at the extent of the damage; we looked at each other and promptly decided it was time to split.

Everyone ran as fast as they could, some heading for home, others running to the sea front where we all intended to meet together later on. In the meantime police and fire brigades came from everywhere. It seems the bomb was heard all over Dublin, even on the south side. I believe each one of us privately thanked God that no one had been hurt.

Halloween of that year was to see the end of my pipe-bomb making for a long time. We had made a number of small bombs and we were carrying them under our coats, heading for St Anne's park. Bags full of weed-killer, sugar, and materials for making fuses and lighting fires bulged in our pockets. One of the gang climbed about twenty feet into a tree and spread some of the explosive mixture on several of the branches. He then lit this and climbed down. It made a lovely sight, the whole tree flaring up and thick grey and white smoke smelling like candyfloss billowing out from under it.

This was the life – no school to go to, money coming in and no responsibilities whatsoever. I was happy and carefree. Later that night we went down to my road and began to light fires in the park at the front of my house with our explosive mixture. We were running out of this and we still had a few bombs left. It was getting late; the rain was beginning to fall and some of us were becoming very drunk and stoned. The more drunk and stoned we were, the more careless we became. I had seen one of the older boys throwing a small pipe-bomb into one of the smaller kids' fires earlier, a crazy stunt that could easily have killed someone. Fortunately most of the younger people had gone home by now. Some of our gang began to waste our explosive weed-killer by burning it on its own. Danny, Jimmy and I still had some copper-bombs and we needed weed-killer for the fuses. We began to run to the fires where the weed-killer was burning and put them out by either stamping on them or smothering them with an old damp rag we had found. I noticed a fire burning over on one side of the park, and I could tell there was weed-killer in it by the colour and the amount of smoke coming from it. Quickly I grabbed the old damp rag we had found and I ran towards the fire, hoping to retrieve the weed-killer for myself. Behind me I could hear some of the gang shouting at me, "Johnny, Johnny, come back! Leave it, Johnny!"

"They just want the weed-killer for themselves," I thought. "Well, this is mine and no one is going to get it from me."

I dived onto the ground about two feet from where the weed-killer was burning and prepared to put the wet rag on it. At that moment I caught sight of Danny and Jimmy running towards me, screaming, "*It's a bomb, Johnny! Get out of there – it's a bomb!*" I still doubted them, but as I looked at the fire I could see a pipe-bomb lying there, the fuse just about spent and the bomb ready to explode. I knew I didn't have time to get up and run away, so instinctively I turned my face and body away and threw myself as hard as I could to one side. I knew that if the bomb exploded in my direction I could be badly injured or even killed.

"God help me," I quickly prayed, and hit the ground hard about four feet away from the bomb. As I did so there was a deafening explosion. I lay motionless on the grass in the park wondering if I was injured or not.

Danny, Jimmy and the rest of the gang came charging over to me. "Johnny, are you OK?" They knelt on the ground beside me and turned me over. "Are you OK, Johnny"?

"I think so," I muttered.

The boys helped me to my feet and examined me. "We thought you were a goner that time. If that pipe had gone in your direction when it exploded you could have been killed, d'ye know that Johnny? Yer an awful eejit, Johnny Edwards – Come on, let's get out of here."

None of us made a big deal out of that episode. We thought we were invincible. Death and serious accidents were things that happened to others, not us. We didn't realise it then but several of the boys with me that night would be dead within a few short years

WALKING FREE

The Stables

In the summer of 1970 we began to hang around at Burns' horse-riding stables, which were situated down by the wooden bridge on the seafront. For a while I dreamt of being a jockey. Danny, Eddie, Ron, Jimmy, George and others, along with me, would go down to the stables whenever we were free. We groomed the horses until their coats were gleaming. Some of us cleaned out their stables and generally kept the yard clean. We prided ourselves on our care of the horses. Danny, Eddie and I were assigned a horse each by Mr Burn to look after and take responsibility for. My horse was called Lancer; he was a bay, about eighteen hands high. When he was younger he had been badly treated and he was terrified of sticks or crops. I never allowed anyone use a crop on him or whip him. I spent hours working with him to gain his trust. Mr Burn noticed how Danny, Eddie and myself were taking good care of the horses and that we fancied ourselves as jockeys. When the stables weren't too busy he would allow us to bring the horses down to the beach to exercise them. We loved these times. Together we would gallop the horses through the shallow water. I would shorten my stirrups and ride like a professional jockey. Oh the thrill of it, our shirts off and the wind blowing through our long hair. We never wore riding hats; they were for learners and we, after all, were potential Grand National winners.

Sometimes Mr Burn let us ride the bigger horses. Aran was one of them. He was a hunter, had a mouth like leather and ran like a steam train. Mr Burn only let you mount Aran if you were a really good rider. I felt tiny on his back. He loved to go down the beach and have a good run. As soon as we hit the beach he would begin to gallop. I was completely powerless to stop him but instead I would stand up on my short stirrups, crouch over like a jockey and enjoy the ride. It was exhilarating, an incredible adrenaline rush! Everyone got out of the way. Even the cars on Dollymount strand had to move aside. This was Aran's run and no one was going to stop him, not even me. "*Yeeeii Haa!*" I would shout with glee. I felt so free and at one with Aran, we were steaming down the beach in total agreement with each other. I would have my shirt off and my long hair would be blowing in the wind behind me. Sometimes I would find myself in tears when we reached the end of the beach. I was not stoned or drunk, yet I was totally happy and free during those gallops. I remember standing up in the stirrups and shouting at the top of my voice with tears running down my face, "Why can't life be like Aran's run? Why can't life be like Aran's run?" He usually got tired by the time he got to the end of the three-mile beach, with both of us out of breath and sweating. We would take it easy coming back home, cooling down as we paced slowly along the hare track at the back of the sand dunes.

Life was good at this time. Danny, Eddie and I met lovely girls at the stables. They didn't take drugs themselves and they tried to get us to stop our drug-taking and our drinking. During this time most of our drug-use was confined to weekends. I was going out with a girl called Susan. We were happy together; she loved horse-riding as much as I did and sometimes we went down the beach together on our horses. We spent some romantic evenings exercising our horses on the beach and then walking them home through the shallow water as the sun set on the horizon. It was the stuff dreams are made of.

Chapter Eight
The Grip of Addiction

Weekend User

On Saturday mornings several of us would meet together to go to buy our drugs. We visited certain chemists in Dublin where we could buy cough bottles over the counter that contained morphine or speed.

It must be remembered that these drugs were not illegal. They were everyday cough-mixture bottles that were fairly easily obtained in the early '70s. They have now either been taken off the market or have had the dangerous drugs taken out of them.

One of these cough bottles was called Doctor Collis Brown's Compound. This had morphine and chloroform in it. We would boil this up in a pot at home if our parents were not in, or else we lit an open-air fire and boiled it outdoors. Once the chloroform was boiled off it was safe to drink. One of my pals nearly died on one occasion when he boiled the mixture in an old coke can. Something from the inside of the can, probably aluminium, melted into the mixture and my friend drank the lot. He broke out in horrible blisters all down his throat. The substance poisoned him, and he spent several weeks in Jervis Street hospital as a result. It was not uncommon for us to drink two or three of these bottles in one night. Then we smoked hash on top of that and ended up stoned out of our heads.

There was one particular cough bottle called Phensydil, which had Ephedrine, a form of "speed", in it. Two bottles of this together with a bit of dope was enough to set us up for the night. We would "speed" around on it, speaking at an incredible rate and running about, unable to stay still for very long. Sometimes I would hallucinate quite badly on Phensydil, especially if I mixed it with Valium and hash.

If we could not get any cough bottles we would buy Benzedrex nasal inhalers. These had Benzedrine speed in them. We would smash these open, take out the cotton wool substance from inside and cut it up. This we swallowed, but first a half-pint of milk had to be drunk to line the stomach. Without the milk the cotton wool cut the inside of the stomach. The cotton wool itself had to be wrapped in white bread, which made it go down easier and softened the taste. Otherwise it made you gag or caused you to vomit it up. It was always unpleasant to have to pick the cotton wool out of our vomit to get it back into us.

Paracodeine cough bottle was one of our favourites. It was full of codeine, a strong painkiller. Some chemists in Dublin would sell us up to five bottles at a time. We often drank two or three bottles of the stuff in one night.

Each of these substances differed in its emotional effects. All of them made us feel good, some better than others. We were usually peaceful and didn't fight or cause trouble when we were using them.

On our days off my pals and I travelled for miles around Dublin looking for new chemists to add to our list. We kept these names to ourselves, as there were a number of people in our area who were beginning to take cough bottles. If the word got out about a new source of supply, too many people would turn up there on Saturday morning. Sometimes the chemist was sold out before we got there or he'd realise what was going on and stop selling them to us. If necessary, we would take a day or two off work and travel around Ireland getting our supply.

Once purchased, the cough bottles or drugs were carefully stashed away. Each of us had a personal hiding place kept secret from everyone else. It was not unknown for someone to follow one of us and steal our stash after we had hidden it. This was a serious offence and if discovered the offender would either be beaten up or banned from hanging around with us. On Saturday night before we met up together, each of us went to his secret stash and drank his own bottles. They all tasted disgusting and once again we often had to catch our vomit in our hands or in a bag and drink it again. The substance was too precious to waste.

Turmoil

Obviously I was in turmoil at this stage. On the one hand I was very happy with Susan, my girlfriend. I loved to walk down the road holding her hand or with my arm around her shoulder. We shared a love of horses and enjoyed looking after them together. On the other hand my job didn't mean very much to me – it was just OK; I could take it or leave it. It was a means of making money; that was all. I didn't like hairdressing. Then there was my home situation, and my attraction to drugs and drink.

One day Susan and I had a terrible argument. She was a good girl who came from a lovely family and wanted nothing whatsoever to do with drugs. Danny's and Eddie's girlfriends were the same. They loved horses and had plans to go to university and better themselves. All of us were given an ultimatum by the girls: either give up drugs and get our acts together or they would leave us.

I was still terribly insecure within myself. My stutter had hardly improved and I felt a terrible pull towards this life of drug-taking. In that life I was somebody. I had an identity, I was accepted and liked, or at least, so I thought – and that was what counted. I so much wanted to be accepted. I did not have much in common with ordinary "good" people, and felt more at ease with my friends who were taking drugs. Inside I was screaming for love. I was not really close to anyone; the gang members had drugs in common, and this replaced real friendship. Yet I did really like some of the gang; we could get on so well and felt so comfortable with each other. I guess all of us were hurting in one way or another. We never talked about it, however; our conversations were limited to drugs, drink, music and having a good time; we never seemed to talk about much else. Only one or two of the boys were interested in chasing women. For the rest of us, drugs and drink were the only things that could satisfy us. Sex was not something we craved after or chased very much. If it came along, it came along; if it didn't, it didn't.

Our bible was the *Mimms Medical Dictionary*. We studied the *Mimms* together and searched everywhere for cough bottles, pills, or other medicines that we could identify as having potential for giving us a good "high". It was not uncommon for us to try a drug we were not sure about just to see if we would get stoned on it. Some of the older lads injected medication as a similar experiment. This was like playing Russian (or *Mimms*) Roulette. Of course I had sworn that I would never inject myself. That would be foolish and I knew better than that, didn't I?

Otherwise I made no conscious decision to go one way or the other; I just allowed circumstances to lead me. Now, for the time being, Susan's ultimatum was being kept on hold.

The "Children of God"

There was another influence in my life at this time. It came in the shape of a group of very happy young people.

The owner of the stables, Mr Burns and his family moved out of the big house that they had occupied at the stables and into a bungalow close by. A group of young people called the "Children of God" took up residence in the big house. They claimed to be born-again Christians and they seemed very happy. They didn't drink or take drugs yet they were always singing, dancing and laughing. They wore brightly coloured clothes and were constantly smiling. Outsiders were welcome to their meetings and occasionally we attended. The Children of God would play guitars, sing and read or share out of the wonderful stories in the Bible. I had never heard anyone speak about God the way they did. He seemed to be very real to them. They were so free and spontaneous in their worship and something felt very right about it. The love of God seemed to shine out of them. I was just a little nervous of them because some local people said that they were a cult and their religion was false. I thought it had more of the reality of God in it than anything I had ever experienced did. I really liked them and I thought they were genuine and sincere.

Cormack, one of the leaders, prayed with me several times and I felt something like electricity move through me. I was left with a sense of peace deep inside. It was a nice feeling, and one I could trust. I was just beginning to feel comfortable with their type of worship when out of the blue they moved out of the big house. I was very disappointed at their departure and never found out where they moved to.

At about the same time Susan told me she wanted to finish our relationship.

"I cannot go out with you as long as you're taking drugs, John. I really care for you but I am getting on with my life. Drugs are not going to be a part of it."

I have had many girlfriends since, but Susan was the first girl that I loved. I could see that she was serious. The strange thing was that this time I didn't argue with her. I knew that I could not cope with reality without the crutch of drugs and drink. The lifestyle surrounding drugs and alcohol abuse had a grip on me now and it was leading me down a very dark and dangerous road. I was a willing captive.

The Druggies

Life was getting darker. All the warning signs were there but I either chose to ignore them or couldn't see them.

Susan was gone; I saw her around the stables still but she was no longer my girl. The Children of God were gone also. Once again all the natural joys of my life seemed to be taken from me. My thoughts returned to the time when Kevin had gone to boarding school, the trees were knocked down in the park, and the rest of the Jinx gang went their own way. Another chapter had now ended in my life, and I had a real sense that another new and dangerous one was beginning.

Some of the older guys began to hang around on the wasteland or field next door to the stables. Their involvement in drugs was deepening, with many of them injecting, and sometimes they could be seen falling and staggering around on the promenade. Some nights they would light fires on the wasteland, where they would drink and take drugs. Other nights they lit their fire on the beach. Sometimes they came into the stables to get water for their syringes out of the tap on the wall outside Lancer's stable, and if I were there they would invite me to join them if I wanted.

"How're ye Johnny; how're ye doin'? If you've nowhere to go later on, come over and have a joint with us. We have a fire lightin' in the hollow of the field next to the stables."

Danny, Eddie and I began meeting up with them some nights, usually with two other friends of ours, George and Jimmy. George lived near me and worked for the Post Office. He was a drinker, very much in love with his Guinness and vodka. He was of stocky build with short black hair. His laugh was contagious and he was part of the core group of our gang. Jimmy was also a local guy. He was full of devilment and he loved lighting fires. On several occasions the long grass down on the beach could be seen burning. Sometimes as much as several hundred yards of it would be in flames. The Royal Dublin Golf Club always called the police or fire brigade if there was trouble or a fire near the golf course. The fire engine would then be heard screaming down the road and along the wooden bridge onto the beach. Next thing Jimmy would be seen crossing the bridge from the opposite direction. He had that little smug grin on his face that said, "That's my fire over there." He was a loveable rogue – you just couldn't help liking him. He was always there if you needed him. He was very handsome and had a fine build and a big mop of curly dark brown hair. He was a true friend, yet he was hard as nails. Along with his drinking habit, at weekends he used to take drugs with us.

Once we began visiting the older lads in the field next to the stables, our own drinking and drug-taking became a little more serious.

I started growing marijuana plants at home. I began by planting seeds that I got from hash we had bought. I placed the seeds in damp cotton wool in our hot press. Daily I checked to see if the seeds had germinated. As soon as they had, I carefully transplanted them to a small pot and placed it on the windowsill in my bedroom.

When the plants had grown to a good size my mam got a bit suspicious.

"John Edwards, what are you growing in those pots?" she asked.

"Tomato plants, ma", I answered.

"And where may I ask you are the tomatoes, John?"

I was an accomplished liar by this time and I also had the gift of the gab. "Well ma, it's like this," I began. "These plants that I am growing are for experimental purposes only. They are all male plants, and as you know male tomato plants do not actually have any fruit."

"So you're taking up gardening, John, are ye?" she said sarcastically.

"I suppose I am in a way, ma," I answered. Then, in order to drive the lie home, I had the cheek to ask her to water them for me if I stayed out over the weekend. I even showed her the fertiliser I was using so that she could put a bit on them now and again.

A few weeks later I came home from work and found her hopping mad. She was fit to kill me. The marijuana plants were a good 3–4 feet tall now and were very bushy. They would soon be ready for harvesting.

"Ye little divil, John Edwards!" she roared at me. "Tomato plants, are they? I'll give you tomato plants. *Marijuana plants* – that is what your plants are. I'll kill you if I get my hands on you! You'll have the police around here raiding us. How dare you! Wait till your father comes home – then you'll know all about it."

I ran upstairs to check my plants, but every one of them was gone. My ma had thrown them all out.

"Where are they, ma?" I shouted. "Where are they? How dare you throw out my plants – they were my property. Where are they?" I screamed at her.

My mother was in tears by now, and she sobbed as she said, "John, if you're not careful you'll end up a drug addict."

"Don't be stupid, ma, I know better than that," I snapped back.

I searched everywhere for the plants and I eventually found them broken and mangled in our coalbunker in the back garden. Only one was still in good condition. The rest I took out and dried before smoking them a few weeks later. That night I stayed in a friend's house in order to avoid a confrontation with my father.

The Drug Squad

On Saturday nights several of the gang travelled into Parnell Square in Dublin city. There was a little hippie club there where dope was smoked regularly. In this place we got friendly with a girl called Liz. She always had lots of Valium, Mogadon and sometimes she had barbiturates called Tuinal. She often gave me Valium and Mogadon; less frequently she gave me Tuinal. These were very strong sleeping capsules. One or two of them would blow the head off me.

One night she said to me, "Have you heard about the new drug centre that has opened up at the back of Jervis Street Hospital, John?"

"Yea I have, Liz. Why do you ask?"

"Well I get my Valium and Mogadon there every week. I just told them I was getting flashbacks from acid and straight away they began to give me 21 blue Valium and seven Mogadon a week."

"You're kidding me, Liz! It couldn't be as easy as that."

"I'm telling you John, it is that easy. Why don't you try it, then you'd have your own weekly supply".

"I will," I answered.

During the following week Eddie and I made an appointment with the doctor in the drug clinic. We arrived fifteen minutes early and sat in the waiting area of the small green prefabricated hut that was Dublin's first drug clinic. We were a little nervous. There were several people who were obviously on drugs waiting to see one of the doctors. These were real drug addicts. I felt sorry for them. Neither Eddie nor I could see that we were becoming just like them.

"John Edwards, the doctor will see you now," the nurse said.

"What's the problem, John?" the doctor asked me. He was

quite young, and he went out of his way to make me feel comfortable. He seemed to be relating to the addicts very well. "Probably had special training at being hip," I thought.

"I'm getting f-flash-backs from taking acid, doctor, and I can't s-sleep properly as a result. I'm very anxious and panicky during the day as well. I was just w-wondering if there is anything that you could give me to h-help me."

He did a few tests on me, checking such things as my blood pressure, temperature and reflexes, and then he told me to sit outside.

Ten minutes later the nurse came out to me and handed me two brown envelopes. One of them contained 21 blue Valium. In the other there were seven Mogadon sleeping tablets. It was as simple as that.

"Come back next week at two o'clock, John, and we'll give you the same again," the nurse said.

"Thank you," I replied

I waited outside for Eddie to see if he had the same luck. He was out in ten minutes.

"Yeah! I got them, Eddie, did you?" I asked.

"Yes I did, and I am getting more every week," Eddie said.

We were jubilant. To celebrate we crossed the road to a pub where we ordered a couple of pints of Guinness. We then took about five blue Valium and a Mogadon each, washing them down with the Guinness. We were as happy as Larry with the success of our little scam. We agreed not to tell anybody about it. If too many people turned up with the same story the doctors might just get suspicious. Eddie and I continued for a long time to return to the drug clinic in Jervis Street. Soon I was going over to the pub and taking all the medication in one go, 21 Valium and seven Mogadon sleeping pills. This was really the beginning of my addiction. I had to start to find other sources to get more Valium. I managed to find several doctors whom I could talk into giving me repeat prescriptions for Valium and there were even several chemists that gave me them over the counter occasionally. I got a bit of a reputation for being able to talk chemists and doctors into giving me prescriptions for almost anything. This was to prove to be my downfall later on.

WALKING FREE

The drug problem in Dublin was growing quickly at this time. Next door to the new centre, Jervis Street Hospital had opened a drug detox ward. Many of the drug addicts from Dublin began to come to the clinic and we were getting to know them. I began buying barbiturates from some of the addicts. Tuinal, Seconal and Nembutal were fairly easy to get. One or two barbs were enough to get me stoned out of my head. These barbs were far stronger than anything else I had taken before and I could buy five for a pound. Two were enough to get me fairly stoned.

Chapter Nine
Near-Death Experience

Black-outs

One winter night I was out with the gang in Clontarf, hanging around as usual in the concrete bus shelter down by the sea front. The shelter was a place where we could get out of the rain and wind and where there also were seats to sit on. My initials can still be seen scratched on the walls. I had taken some barbs and mixed them with "Marie Celeste", a cheap sherry. Barbs and alcohol make up a very dangerous mixture that can not only kill you very easily, but can also cause you to get quite violent. It certainly had a violent effect on me. This particular night Bob and I had a terrible fight. Bob was a friend of mine when we were sober. He was a huge guy, a good six or seven inches taller than me and about twice my weight. He was all muscle with not a bit of fat on him. Like a lot of little guys, I was inclined to pick fights when I was drunk or stoned with bigger guys, usually much bigger guys. By now I was beginning to get memory blackouts when I was drunk or stoned and I don't remember what happened on this occasion. My friends told me that I would not give in and kept kicking and trying to hit him. Then I was knocked to the ground and Bob began to kick the left side of my head full force with his boots. This resulted in the right side of my face smashing against the pebble-dashed wall of the bus shelter. I was knocked unconscious. My friends panicked when they saw a river of blood come out from under my head. They all ran away and left me there. I could easily have died from loss of blood.

WALKING FREE

I lay unconscious in the shadows of the bus shelter for I don't know how long, until finally a bus stopped to let a passenger off. The bus conductor noticed the blood oozing out from the shadows of the bus shelter and onto the road. I thank God that he went in and had a look to see what the source of the blood was. I was still lying unconscious in the same position my so-called friends had left me in. The bus conductor called to the driver for help and between the two of them they carried me onto the bus. They drove me straight into the accident and emergency department of Jervis Street Hospital. I was quickly put on a trolley and brought into the treatment room. They discovered that my right ear had been sliced in two and I had bad gashes on both sides of my face. They could not revive me; so between giving me x-rays, stitching my head up and sewing my ear back together again, they also had to pump my stomach because I was obviously very stoned and drunk.

I did not become conscious again until the following afternoon. One of the doctors then told me about what had happened the night before and how the bus had brought me into the hospital.

"Somebody up there is looking after you, John," the doctor said. "You lost a lot of blood, and how your skull is not fractured I do not know. Whoever did this could have killed you. Do you remember the bus bringing you in to us, John?"

"No, Doctor," I answered. To this day I cannot remember any of it. My face was a mess and some of my hair had to be shaved off so that the doctors could stitch my head. One of my eyes was covered in white gauze and a patch. Most parts of my face, especially my eyes and cheeks, were a mixture of black, blue and yellow. The one eye that was not covered was three-quarters closed because it was so swollen. Soon after I spoke to the doctor two detectives came into the ward. They said they knew who had done this to me and all they needed from me was a statement and they would do him for attempted murder. I never said a word about Bob. I wasn't even sure if he was the culprit because of my drugged blackout, but even if I had been sure there is an unwritten law that you don't grass-up your mates. The police pestered me for over half-an-hour.

"John, this Bob has hurt a lot of people and he could have killed you last night. We need someone to give a statement to us about him. Then we can do something about it."

"I don't know who has done this to me, honest to God, I don't know; I c-cannot remember a thing about it. Will yiz just l-leave me alone – I'm not feeling very well." They knew that there was no way I was going to tell them so they eventually left.

I had some time on my own once the police were gone. "Some friends they were," I thought to myself. "I could have been killed last night and not one of them stayed to see if I was OK. Loyalty amongst friends – there is no such thing." I felt very lonely and let down that day and was quite disappointed in the lads.

We used to look after one another; we used to watch each other's backs; we used to care, but not any more. Drugs, drink and addiction had taken us over. We were no longer interested in helping each other. Real friendship and caring was something other people had, not me: not the gang, not the lads. We were just out for ourselves.

I felt cornered, unable to get away from my own thoughts. The reality of my way of life was coming home to me. I didn't like it any more and I wanted something better, although I didn't know how or where to make a change.

"Please God, if you're there, help me," I cried to myself as I lay on my bed all bandaged and stitched up. I was broken inside and out.

I must have dozed off because the next thing I heard was someone whispering, "John, John, can you hear me, are you awake?" I lifted my head slightly and turned it so that I could see who it was through my swollen and half-closed left eye. It was my father. He was ashen-faced.

"Oh God, just look at the mess your face is in . . . " He lifted his hand up and stroked my hair in a rare gesture of affection. "Your hair is all caked in blood as well, John." I could hear his voice breaking. He quickly pulled himself together and began to take a different tone.

"John," he said, "everyone knows who did this to you. The word is out on the streets." My dad was extremely upset to see me in this state and angry with me because of the lifestyle I was living. He gave me twenty cigarettes and began to plead with me to change my ways.

"I'll try, dad," I promised. He left the hospital that morning with tears in his eyes. I knew I was breaking his heart and the hearts of the rest of my family. I had more pressing issues though, that needed to be dealt with; I was beginning to feel sick from withdrawals. I called a nurse and it wasn't long before the hospital had sorted me out with a cure. *After all, I was registered in Jervis Street Drug Clinic as having a drug problem . . .*

I was moved to the new detox ward that was attached to the drug clinic, where I was given enough medication to keep me sane. One or two of my friends came to see me and they brought me in some more Valium and even some whiskey to keep me going. One of my pals brought me a bottle of orange that was spiked with ethyl alcohol. I stayed here for a week or so before they discharged me. I met some older junkies there, some of whom were in terrible condition; they too were having drugs brought in by friends and relatives.

I got a very cool reception from my family when I returned to the house. My lifestyle was upsetting them. I felt bad about this but couldn't find it within myself to do anything about it. I made promises to try to stay off drugs, but as usual it wasn't long before I was back using again.

Chapter Ten
Losing my Grip

Moran's Hotel

Music was a very important part of our lives. The albums of bands such as Pink Floyd, the Rolling Stones, Black Sabbath and Hawkwind were playing constantly on our record players and reel-to-reel stereos at night. For live music Moran's Hotel in Talbot Street was a popular venue. The Boomtown Rats, among others, began their careers there. Most Tuesday, Thursday and Saturday nights we could be found in Moran's, and inevitably drink and drugs were a vital part of the evening.

A guy I met in Moran's told me that if I opened the barbiturate capsules and put the horrible-tasting barbiturate powder in very hot water, then drank it down in one go, the effects of the drug would come on me in ten minutes instead of the usual fifteen or twenty. I had begun to want a more instant hit; the quicker the drug or drink came on, the better. I was, at this stage, losing interest in myself; my personal hygiene standards had dropped and I could sometimes smell myself. I began to take more days off work. I made any excuse to get out of it. Sometimes I got friends to phone up the shop and cause a bomb-scare. As a result the shop would have to close, and I was free for the day. My pals would be waiting down the end of Wicklow Street for me. We thought it was great fun. We had no sense of responsibility whatsoever and we were becoming totally selfish. We began to get to know many of the addicts in the city. Most of these were injecting their drugs. I had promised myself never to inject drugs; I knew that if I started to inject them there would be no going back for me. Addiction seems to have a life of its own; it slowly drags you down to a place where it totally dominates you. Values you once held highly go. Standards of hygiene go. Self-respect goes. What is right or wrong doesn't matter as much as it used to. Promises you have made to yourself begin to get broken. Very soon I was to break the vow I had made to myself.

One night I was sitting on a public seat across the road from the front gates of Trinity College. A well-known Dublin addict called Finto came and sat beside me.

"How's it goin', Johnny?" he asked me.

"Oh I'm fed up, Finto; I'm broke and I don't feel very well."

" I've got some barbs if you want some," said Finto. "3 grain Tuinal. Here, I'll lay a couple on ye, that will cheer ye up."

"Thanks Finto, I really appreciate that."

"No problem, Johnny. Here, do you want to borrow me works as well?"

"I don't inject, Finto. I'll go into the toilets in Trinity and get some hot water to take – that will bring them on quicker."

"Johnny, let an old addict give you some advice. Don't ever start injecting, OK?"

"I don't intend to, Finto."

Finto and I went into the toilets in Trinity and I took my horrible-tasting hot water and barbiturates. Finto then took out his "works", filled the syringe with water from the tap and opened two of the barbiturate capsules, emptying them one at a time into his water-filled syringe. He then gave it a good shake and asked me to hold it for him. I knew that my fix would take another ten minutes to make an effect and I was fascinated watching this old addict go through the process of injecting himself. As I held the syringe for him, it was strange how immediately I felt attracted to it and the power that it had to bring on the drugs almost instantly. By now Finto had taken his jacket off and had rolled up his sleeve; he had his belt wrapped around his upper arm just above his elbow and was busy pumping his arm up and down trying to work up a vein to inject into. I could see in the dim light of the toilet that his arm was badly track-marked. I was impressed; these were like stripes to a soldier, or war wounds; in some sick way they commanded respect from me for him.

"Hey, Johnny, snap out of it and give me the works. Ye look like you're hypnotised or something. Have your barbs come on yet?"

"No, they haven't; it'll be a few minutes yet." Finto took the works from me, shook it again, and then held it up to the light as if he were a doctor and squirted out some liquid until all the air was out of the syringe. He tightened the belt around his arm and positioned the syringe above a vein that was slightly bulging. He pumped his arm a couple more times and then slipped the needle in under his skin.

"Got it," he said, as dark blood came into the tip of the syringe. He slowly plunged the liquid into his arm then released his grip on the belt. Finto let out a deep sigh of satisfaction as he did so. "Aah! That's better." He sat down on the toilet-seat, almost falling as he did so. I noticed that he didn't even clean the syringe out before we left; he put the cap on over the orange needle and slipped it into his pocket. We walked out again onto the cold Dublin streets. There was warmth in the pit of my stomach: the barbs were coming on now but not with the same rush that I could see Finto enjoying earlier. I began to think that maybe I'd try to inject just once to see what it would be like. Just as quickly I pushed the thought out of my mind and I became lost in my drug-induced stupor. I was happy again, for a while anyway.

One Saturday night Danny and I were in the Sheds pub on the Clontarf Road in Dublin. We were having a few pints before we went to Moran's. Danny had got hold of some strong opiates called Palfium. Earlier in the night he had opened up to me and told me that he had begun "shooting-up" his drugs. I wasn't really all that surprised; many of the gang had progressed onto harder drugs and were now injecting.

I asked Danny to give me an injection of Palfium.

"Johnny, are you sure that you want to?"

"Yes I'm sure, Danny," I responded. "I've been thinking about it for a while and I know it may be the wrong thing to do but I want to try it. D-don't worry Danny, I am not going to get addicted; I'm just going to t-try it. I want to see what it's like."

"OK, Johnny. Let's go up to the toilet and do it now."

I could feel my legs shaking as we went upstairs. I was excited and apprehensive at the same time. The brown door at the top of the stairs led into the toilet. We were relieved to see that it was empty. I knew the drill for injecting drugs as I had seen many of my friends shooting up during the previous few years.

We let the cold tap run for a while, thinking that somehow this made the water more pure or clean. Danny then filled the syringe with water. While he was doing this I crushed two Palfium tablets between the folds of a piece of cardboard torn from a box of Friendly matches, and poured the crushed powder into the syringe as Danny held it still. He injected half of the mixture into himself first. He seemed to know what he was doing and the effects of the drug hit him instantly. Then it was my turn.

I was extremely nervous. Beads of perspiration came out on my forehead and I could feel a trickle of sweat run down my back. I rolled back the sleeve of my shirt and pumped my veins up by squeezing my arm above the elbow. They swelled up big and stood out on my arm as the blood pressure built up.

"Your veins are an addict's dream, Johnny," Danny said. "They're like ropes."

When I was ready I told him to go ahead. It didn't bother me too much that some of his blood was mixed with the water and Palfium.

Danny pressed the tip of the green spike against the inside of my arm near my elbow. The needle slipped in and I could feel it sort of pop as it went through the wall of my virgin vein. My heart was thumping and my mind was racing. I knew that I shouldn't be doing this. I had sworn to myself that I would never do it. I was supposed to know better. Danny pulled the plunger back, and dark red blood told us that he had hit the vein.

"Fasten your seat belt, Johnny, you're going for a ride."

With that he plunged the Palfium into my arm. Immediately

LOSING MY GRIP

I was caught up in the most amazing feeling I had ever had. I was high as a kite.

"Oh Danny, this is fantastic!" I said. "Oh wow! I never thought I could feel this good."

Danny pulled the plunger back a couple of times, filling the syringe with blood, and then he flushed it back into my vein. Finally he withdrew the needle from my vein. I bent my arm and held a bit of toilet paper to the puncture to stop any bleeding that might occur.

"Come on, Johnny, there's somebody coming – let's get out of here."

I was oblivious to everything, I felt so good. I just wanted to be everybody's friend. Danny rushed me out through the toilet door and down the stairs. Grabbing our jackets from the bar we went out into the cold air. We jumped on a bus and headed into Trinity College to score some hash and hang out in the common room. Later we travelled up to Zero's Night Club near Capel Street. Phil Lynnot from Thin Lizzy turned up that night. He and Brush Shields jammed together with a couple of other musicians. Danny and I shot up some more Palfium. I cannot remember getting home.

Crisis

In the '70s drugs were fairly easy to come by. The Drug Squad was new in Dublin and Detective Inspector Dinny Mullins and his crew were beginning to show a lot of interest in our gang in Clontarf. They didn't yet know much about us or about how we got our drugs; indeed, we got them in many different ways.

We made up our own prescriptions from cut-down A4 paper. Then with Letraset we put a doctor's name and address on the top of each one. One of the lads then forged a script for Palfium, Diconal or barbiturates or whatever else we wanted. These were fairly easy to exchange in a chemist shop. On top of this, some of us travelled far and wide to find doctors who would give us prescriptions for hard drugs. We kept their identities a secret, as we had with the unsuspecting chemists. I used my skills as a barber to get into one doctor's good books. A lady doctor in Clontarf got me to cut her husband's hair now and again. He was a retired police sergeant. Instead of charging her for the haircut I asked her to give me prescriptions for Diconal or barbiturates. This she gladly did. Unfortunately she was later struck off the Register of Doctors.

Our local chemist knew me from when I was a little baby; he knew that I was a drug addict and he genuinely felt sorry for me and wanted to help. I would go into his shop for a chat and over a period of time he began to bring me into the back of the premises. Usually the kettle was put on and out came the chocolate digestives.

"How are you getting on, John?" he would ask. "You're a good lad, and your parents have given you a good upbringing. My heart is broken to see the state you're in. You need to get some professional help before you do yourself some real damage or these drugs will kill you, son."

We usually talked for a while and then before I left I would ask him for something to take my sickness away. He knew when I was sick from withdrawal and he always helped me out with some barbiturates or opiates.

"Here you are, John," he would say as he handed me the drugs, sometimes with tears in his eyes. "Now promise me you will get help."

"I promise, Mr Cronin," was my customary reply as I left the shop. I respected him; he was a nice man and he helped me a lot. I never abused his kindness, but only visited him when I was desperate.

Syringes were harder to come across. We sometimes shared one syringe between as many as ten of us for a couple of weeks. Often the needle got blunt so we sharpened it with sandpaper or even by rubbing it against a wall. To clean it we put thin wire down the middle of the needle to remove anything that might be blocking it. Then we'd burn the needle-part of the syringe with a match or Zippo lighter, which we thought would sterilise it. I still have some black marks in my arms from the soot that came off the syringes.

My health began to suffer at this time. I left my job in Lionel's hairdressers. I had qualified as a colourist and cutter and was very good at it but my heart was not in the work. My sister Evelyn gave me a job in her salon in Clontarf. She was aware of my drug-taking and drinking, as were all my family. While I worked for her I tried to pull myself together and cut down on the drugs. Some of Evelyn's clientèle tried to help me. Somehow they all loved me, and most of them knew that I was an addict and alcoholic. They would encourage me and pray for me to get better. "Oh John, you're such a nice fellow, please try to get your life together . . ." Many of them had Masses said for me. In return I was very fond of them, and in some ways it was they who helped me to keep going.

One Friday evening after a busy day in the salon I was feeling particularly nervous and agitated. I went out to the shop next door and bought myself a bottle of cheap sherry. This would usually calm my nerves down. I walked through the salon with the intention of drinking the sherry in the back toilet. I had mastered the art of drinking a full medium-sized bottle of the sweet liquid in one go, opening my throat and pouring it down in under a minute. On this occasion I got as far as ten feet from the toilet when I collapsed into a withdrawal fit. The bottle broke on the floor of the shop, spilling the contents. My whole body shook and quivered, and while frothing at the mouth I bit my tongue. I regained consciousness about two minutes later, feeling like a bomb had gone off in my head. Many of the women who were having their hair done were in shock, but some of them ran to try and help me.

Evelyn got me a taxi to take me home. My mam was in a terrible state when I arrived; she was nearly out of her mind with worry about me. During the fit Evelyn had noticed the needle marks in my arm and she told my parents about them. I was a blithering mess when they brought me inside, and I was still partially in the fit. My mother couldn't handle it; she almost took a nervous breakdown right there in front of my eyes.

"My boy is dead," she kept saying, "my boy is dead. My first boy is dead."

"I'm okay, ma," I said, moving up close to her. "Look, I'm okay, ma."

She didn't seem to notice me. There was a strange stare in her eyes.

"John," my dad cried, "look at what your drug-taking and drinking is doing to us. We love you son, we love you and we've been trying to help you but we cannot take any more of this."

Eamon and Michael became very upset. Their mother and brother were breaking down right in front of them.

"What's wrong with John, da?" Michael asked.

"He is sick, son," my father answered.

"Will he be all right, da?" Eamon asked anxiously. My two younger brothers were getting bigger and older now. They were also getting fed up with my carry-on, but on this night they were genuinely worried for me. I wanted to comfort them and let them know that their brother and mother were going to be just fine.

"Come on, Alice," my da said, "come on, Eamon and Michael. Let's go out for a drive. You stay in, John, now do you hear me? Don't go out anywhere."

"I won't, da, I promise." I was left on my own in the house. My brain was numbed from the fit I had taken but once again I began to take stock of the situation.

What had happened to me? I was completely out of control. I never planned to get addicted; how could I be so stupid? Me, John Edwards, an addict! I had thought that I was in control. How could I do this to my mother? I was frightened at the state of mind she was in; I had had no idea that I was grieving and hurting her so much. By this time my descent into addiction had become more and more obvious to them. I had overdosed several times already and had been in hospital overnight for observation on one occasion. My parents had to watch me doing this to myself. How could I have been so selfish and uncaring? I was doing the same things my da had done except I was worse than he had ever been.

"God, please help my ma; please let her be OK," I prayed.

I decided to try to do something to pull myself together. I would speak to my parents about it when they came home later.

My mother was in better form when she and the others returned later that night.

"Are you OK now, John?" she said, as she cuddled me.

"Yea ma, I am OK."

LOSING MY GRIP

When everyone was in the room I apologised to them for upsetting them so much. I also told them that I intended to go into hospital to seek help

"Will you, John?" my ma said, and there was hope in her eyes again. That funny expression had gone out of them.

"I'll make inquiries in the morning," I said. "I promise."

I got my mother on her own a bit later and asked her to give me a few Valium to help me sleep and to keep the fits away. As usual she was willing to help and gave me three of her 5mg tablets. She had seen me take severe withdrawals in the past and knew the danger of my taking convulsions, which is why she gave me the Valium.

Chapter Eleven
One Flew Over the Cuckoo's Nest

Psychiatric Hospital

Next day my dad helped me make inquiries about a hospital bed for me to do a detox. There were no beds available in the Jervis Street Detox Unit. The only place where I might possibly get a bed quickly was in St Brendan's Psychiatric Hospital. This was popularly known as Grange Gorman, after the area in which it is situated. It was the most notorious "loony bin" in Ireland, but I had to accept it. My family was relying on my keeping my promise to get help.

They were willing to take me in that very afternoon. Nervously I began to pack some clothes and toiletries.

"Ma, I hate going into this place," I said. "It's a nut-house. Am I c-crazy? Do you think I am losing my mind, ma?"

"Of course you're not, John. You've just got a few problems to sort out; then you'll be fine."

"Are you sure, ma?"

"Of course I am, John. Now don't worry, son, you'll be OK. We'll come in and see you every day."

"Give us another few Valium to keep me going till I get there, will you, ma?"

I was genuinely frightened. I was going to a nut-house: did this mean I was losing my marbles? I wasn't sure about anything any more.

My dad drove me to the hospital that evening. St Brendan's is just off the North Circular Road, not far from Dublin Zoo. The building was old, grey and spooky-looking. It was exactly what you would expect a psychiatric hospital to look like. I was being admitted to stay in Unit Q. When we arrived there was no one to meet us. My father and I climbed some old, depressing-looking grey stairs to the first floor. There was a big wooden door at the top of the stairs, with a notice indicating that this was the entrance to Unit Q. We tried the handle, only to discover that the door was locked.

"Strange," my dad exclaimed.

At that moment the door opened and a man dressed in civilian clothes stood before us.

"Hello; you must be Mr Edwards. Come in, we've been expecting you."

Once we were inside the door he closed it and turned the key in the lock. I was frightened, and even my dad seemed a little nervous.

"Give me your bag, John," the nurse said. "Come in here to this room and we'll check you in."

After I had been searched for drugs, they gave me a pair of striped pyjamas and an old hospital dressing gown to wear.

"Here, John, put these on. You are not allowed to wear your clothes in here for the first week or so. When you are feeling better we'll give them to you."

I didn't resist them at all. The fight was gone out of me. I was sick, weary and very afraid.

"Come on down to the ward, John, and I'll show you your bed," the nurse said.

"I'll be off now, John," my dad said. "Your mam and I will come in to see you tomorrow." He looked at me with his piercing dark brown eyes. It was like he was trying to see right into my mind and say, "I know how you feel, John. I have been in hospital too." He shook my hand very hard and said, "You did the right thing coming in. I'll see you tomorrow."

My da and I didn't hug any more. He was becoming like a stranger to me. Sometimes I didn't know what to say to him. I still longed for him to be proud of me; I still so much wanted to be his friend and to let him know that I loved him.

"Take care, son," he added. He waved as the nurse unlocked the big door to let him out of the ward, and then he was gone.

I felt so vulnerable and alone after he left. I looked around me. The place was old, and the high ceilings and cream-painted concrete walls created a slight echo with every sound. I could hear voices coming from the ward.

"Come on, John, let's get you settled into your bed." The male nurse led me to the ward. I carried a bag with my bottle of Lucozade, some fruit and 100 Major cigarettes my father had bought for me. We passed several people, some of whom were in their ordinary clothes. Others wore only pyjamas. I noticed one young man dressed in a grey herringbone suit, his thick brown hair badly cut and sticking out in all directions. He was making strange grunting and groaning noises. "That is Robert," the nurse said. "He has lived in here for years. He is deaf and dumb."

Then we passed a tall, skinny fellow with long, black, unkempt hair and staring eyes. He was in his early thirties. A sweeping brush rested on his folded arms, and as I passed near him his searching, staring dark eyes disarmed me in my nervous state. I knew instinctively that I would have to sort this guy out soon if I was to have any peace during my stay here. He hissed menacingly at me and said, "Hey you! If you mess with anyone in here I'll sort you out. Keep all the rules, stay out of my way and do your chores and you'll be OK."

"That's Billy," the nurse said. "Don't mind him, he's harmless; he thinks he's in charge of the ward."

I felt in need of some medication. Both the culture shock of coming into this terrible place, and the withdrawals I was beginning to experience, were getting to me.

"Nurse, when do I get my medication? I feel terrible."

"The doctor will be around in an hour or so to see you, John. He will prescribe you something then. In the meantime here is your bed; have a lie down on it until he comes."

He directed me to a bed in a corner at the end of the ward. The bed was a horrible cream colour, the same as the walls. It looked as if a patient had picked the colour scheme in here. A big old-fashioned radiator stood on one side of the bed, painted light-green; on the other side was a small varnished wooden locker, on top of which were an ash tray, a plastic beaker and a container with water in it. I put my few belongings in the cupboard, filled my plastic beaker with Lucozade and sat on the bed to wait for the doctor.

I looked around the ward. Some people lay on their beds sleeping, others sat alone or huddled in small groups talking quietly together. A couple of older men just kept wandering around muttering to themselves. An old lady was sitting with Robert, the deaf mute. Her hands were bandaged. I later learned that this was his mother, and that her hands were bandaged because of rat bites she got in her house.

The doctor came and prescribed Sodium Amytal for me. I was addicted to barbiturates and Valium and this was the treatment for it. I was given quite a high dosage to start with, which knocked me out for several hours. The doctor also gave me Tegratol, which was designed to prevent me taking withdrawal fits. When I woke up it was time for my night medication.

Soon I was asleep again, remaining unconscious until around midnight, when something disturbed me. I woke up, vaguely aware of a strange grunting noise, and wondering where I was. Dazed from the high dosage of medication, I had difficulty making anything out.

I raised myself on one elbow and looked across the dimly lit ward. I could not believe what I saw. One of the old men was sexually abusing Robert right in front of my eyes. They were only about twenty feet away from me. Poor Robert was grunting and groaning in protest at what the old guy was doing to him. He was trying vainly to push him away. Hastily I climbed out of bed and rushed towards them.

"Get out of here, you dirty old pervert, before I smack you one! Leave Robert alone." The old guy looked totally startled and scampered frightened back to his bed. Someone shouted across the ward at me, "You're not meant to be out of your bed. Get back in before I come and sort you out."

I peered into the shadows, trying to make out who it was had shouted. It was Billy, staring back at me with his piercing eyes. "Get back into your bed," he hissed at me angrily.

I marched right over to him and said, "Billy, don't you ever tell me what to do. If you speak to me like that again I'll knock the living daylights out of you – do you hear me?" I pointed my finger right into his face. He shrunk back in his bed and there was now a frightened look in his eyes. I began to feel sorry for him.

"Hey Billy, you and I can be friends," I said as I held out my hand to shake his.

"OK, John," he answered.

"What's going on over there?" a voice said, coming from behind me. It was one of the nurses.

"John, what's the problem? You shouldn't be out of your bed."

"Can I speak to you in private, nurse?"

"Yes," he replied, and he led me to the office.

He sat on his office chair and I explained to him exactly what I had seen the old man do to Robert. "He was being sexually abused," I said. "Did you not hear what was going on?"

I could not believe what he said to me next.

"Of course we know what is going on. That guy you saw is an old man and that is one of the few pleasures he has left in his life. Don't you interfere in this."

"Are you crazy?" I cried. "He was s-sexually abusing Robert – you c-can't allow that to continue!"

"John, you're a patient in here, you're in for your drug addiction; what happened tonight is none of your business. Now get back to bed and go to sleep before there's trouble."

I couldn't believe what I was hearing. I was totally confused and upset. I went back to bed and lay there. I cried the whole night, wondering what kind of a place I was in. The thought ran through my head, "Robert gets sexually abused and nobody cares. I am not listened to because I am only a drug addict and a patient in Unit Q in a mental hospital . . . " During that night I made a decision that one day I would speak up for people who have not got a voice for themselves.

The next day I was totally depressed and sick with withdrawals. I felt like I was cracking up. I could not handle what had happened on the previous night with Robert. I tried to talk to other staff about it but they also told me to mind my own business. The shock of coming into a psychiatric hospital, particularly one as morbid as this, along with the effects of coming off drugs and witnessing the abuse, was just too much for me. Some time during that day I snapped. I cannot remember a thing about it. I was told afterwards that I had been shouting and swinging my arms wildly around myself. The first thing I do recall was becoming conscious and finding myself lying in a semi-dark, square-shaped room. I was totally naked. There were no windows, and the floor was hard and cold but with some unusual give in it. I got to my feet wondering what I was doing naked and in this strange, empty place. There was one dim light in the ceiling. I walked around the room and felt the walls with my hands. The walls were a horrible brown colour, and as I ran my hands over them feeling the soft surface with my fingertips and palms, it suddenly struck me that I was in a padded cell.

"No!" I screamed, horrified. "Let me out of here! I'm not crazy, you're m-making a mistake – please help me! Somebody, please help me!" The sound of my words seemed to stay in the room, unable to carry any further. My words were prisoners with me in this horrible place.

I fell down in the corner on my face and cried like a baby. What was happening to me? How did I end up in here? These places were only for crazy people. I was never meant to end up in a padded cell.

After what seemed like hours, the door was opened and my pyjamas were thrown in to me. "Here, John, put these on." Two male nurses came in and brought me to my bed. They gave me my medication and then left me lying there.

I couldn't handle the situation at all. "I have not been able to handle life or reality since I was twelve or thirteen and I can't handle it now," I thought.

That night when the medication tray came around I stole a bottle of Largactyl from the bottom of it. This was easy to do, as nobody paid much attention to us. I knew the exact spot where the nurse gave out the medication. There was a wall next to the spot that I could hide beside. When the patients came and lined up for their medication I got myself ready. I could see the bottle of Largactyl on the bottom of the trolley. The nurse turned to give medication to one of the patients; I pounced on the bottle of Largactyl and ran into the toilet. I opened the bottle as quickly as I could and took several deep swigs from it. Then I put the bottle under my pyjama top and returned to where the nurse was giving out the medication. Once again when she wasn't looking I replaced the bottle on the bottom of the trolley. I then went to the end of the queue and got my own prescribed medication. I knew I had taken enough to knock me out of reality for a couple of days.

I wandered around in a stoned haze for two or three days after that. Nobody bothered me and I didn't bother anyone.

Helping Hurting People

The next week was far better than the first few days. I settled into the routine of the place. The nurses said to me that I should not have been put in St Brendan's.

"You're not psychologically sick, John," they said. "You're a drug addict and an alcoholic. You need to go to rehab." It was a great comfort to know that I was not crazy.

Many of the patients began to look to me and speak to me about their problems. One of these was Gerry, who was about 30 years of age, an alcoholic who had recently taken a nervous breakdown. He was a really nice fellow and until his breakdown had been the manager of a pub near the Donaghmede Shopping Centre on the north side of Dublin. Gerry and I became great hospital friends, encouraging one another and giving one another hope for the future. He did not seem to me to be very sick at all.

"You'll be going home soon, Gerry," I kept telling him.

"Yeah, I am feeling good," he assured me.

One morning I awoke to find Gerry in a terrible state. He was crying his eyes out and I could not console him. Finally he told me that the doctor had just informed him he was being sent down to the lock-up ward. Everyone spoke with fear and dread about this ward. Seemingly it was a place where they locked you in your room and took most of your privileges from you.

"John," he confided, "I cannot handle going in there – I'll kill myself if they send me down. Please help me."

I was genuinely upset for him. It is amazing how close you get to people in psychiatric hospitals.

"What can I do, Gerry? How can I help you?"

"Don't let them take me out of here," he answered.

I promised him that I would help him.

That afternoon, with "Angry Billy" as my right-hand man, I spoke confidentially to each of the patients in Unit Q.

"The word is they're going to take G-Gerry down to the lock-up ward. We don't think it is right and we are going to make a protest. If they won't listen to us we will have to s-stop them taking Gerry. Will you help us stop them taking him?" One by one most of them agreed.

At one stage I had to stop Billy threatening some of the patients with violence if they didn't help. "They don't have to help unless they want to – OK, Billy?"

"Ok, John."

Many of the guys who agreed to help were still in their pyjamas, and some were recovering from serious nervous breakdowns. We were a motley crew of about twelve; the "Dozy Dozen" I called us. We were old, young, deaf, dumb, addicted and crazy. We didn't know much between us, but we did know that no one was going to take Gerry to a lock-up ward tonight, not if we could help it. I arranged it that when the staff came for him everyone was to watch me and wait for the word to attack if necessary. I was hoping the nurses wouldn't come for him before I had taken my evening medication. My luck was in, as it turned out, and about an hour after teatime medication had been delivered, the staff came to get Gerry.

They cleared out his locker for him and told Gerry to get a move on and not to cause any bother. Gerry began to cry and pleaded with them not to take him. I rushed over to them and told them to leave him alone.

"John, this has nothing to do with you – get out of the way."

They began to pull Gerry to his feet as he pleaded with them. He was terrified. I knew this was a crazy situation and that I might get into trouble for what I was about to do. They hadn't listened to me in Robert's sexual abuse case, but I was determined they would listen to me this time.

ONE FLEW OVER THE CUCKOO'S NEST

I looked over my shoulder. There were the lads, all ready for me to give the word. Billy was at the head of them all, with that funny look in his eyes again, but this time he was smiling.

"Come on, boys," I shouted. As I did so I jumped on the staff and pulled them off Gerry. "Run, Gerry, hide somewhere!"

The staff members were trying to get past me. I punched one of them, and as I did the lads jumped in. We overpowered the staff very quickly and pushed them out through the door, which they had left unlocked for Gerry's removal. Once they were outside, Gerry came out of hiding and sat shaking on his bed.

"Thanks, John," he said. "I am not crazy, I promise you I am really not crazy; I am just getting over my breakdown."

"I know, Gerry," I said. "We'll look after you."

The staff had vanished down the stairs. We had the ward to ourselves. I looked at the Dozy Dozen. Their eyes were shining and they all had satisfied smiles on their faces. "This is the first time I have seen these people alive since I came in here," I thought.

"Well done boys," I said. "That is round one over. I don't know w-where they've gone but they'll be back. Are you ready?" I had no idea that hospitals like St Brendan's had bouncers – I just never thought about it – but I was about to find out.

After about twenty minutes I heard a sudden rush of people coming up the stairs. All the patients scattered except Billy. Then the door came crashing open and a gang of heavies burst in behind what looked like a mattress with handles on the back of it. They charged down the corridor next to the ward. Billy fell to the ground and they ran over him. Picking him up, they shouted, "Where's Edwards?"

"I don't know," answered Billy.

I ran and jumped into somebody's bed, pulling the covers over my head in an attempt to hide. The heavies searched every room, every nook and cranny, until they found me.

"I've got him – I've got him!" shouted one of the heavies. Several of them rushed to where I was and dragged me out of the bed. They gave me a good hiding, kicking and punching me in the body. Then they plunged two huge yellow syringes into my hips, one for each side, and injected me with some substance. Immediately I was disabled. My legs went limp and lifeless. I was put back into my bed and given a big dose of medication.

There was nothing more said to me about the situation. Gerry was kept in the ward for a couple more days and then he was taken down to the lock-up ward. I never saw or heard from him again.

The next morning I was still very stoned from the extra medication given to me on the previous night. I was also bruised and hardly able to walk. Two of the male nurses came and brought me to the dentist. I had a hole between my two front teeth that needed filling. I asked no questions as I was positioned in the dentist's chair and had my two front teeth extracted. To this day I do not know why they did not try to save them.

I spent my remaining days in St Brendan's being a model patient. I did not say a word about the continuing sexual abuse or any of the other mistreatment of patients.

The staff eventually gave me my clothes back and told me that I could do some of the patients' shopping for them. I would get a shopping list from the patients and then walk down to a little shop on the North Circular Road. This shop also sold sherry and wine, so on every visit I purchased a bottle of cheap sherry. I would then go down a back alley on the way back to the hospital and drink the sherry in one go. I would also purchase a packet of mints thinking that they would take the smell of drink away. Nobody ever challenged me about my drinking.

I would sometimes visit the girls' ward downstairs from our ward. There was one particular girl there that I was very fond of. I could speak to her without stuttering and look her straight in the eye when I spoke to her. Her name was Evelyn and she was in the hospital because she could not yet handle living outside after an accident she had had. One day she was visiting her friend who worked in her local chip shop. She was sitting up on the counter talking to her friend when all of a sudden she slipped and went headfirst into the boiling oil. Her nose and cheeks were burned off. There was a gaping hole where her nose had been and the skin of her cheeks was like thin stretched leather. She would say to me, "I used to be beautiful before my accident, John. I got confidence from how I looked; now I have got to find the confidence to live a normal life from another source. I pray and ask God to help me find the strength to live outside again and handle the stares and whispered remarks from people."

"I see beauty in you, Evelyn," I told her. "I see you use your compassion to encourage the other patients. You are gentle, not bitter. You're nice to talk to. You have an acceptance and honesty about your circumstances that I just do not see in others. I don't feel judged by you because I am an addict and an alcoholic. There are not many that I feel so comfortable around."

She said something to me that helped me more than all the doctors and nurses in the hospital together. "John," she said, "you must be one of the nicest people I have ever met. Nobody else – not even my family – comes to see me in here. You have encouraged me so much and given me the strength to hopefully one day live outside again. You have tremendous potential to help others, John, and I believe that one day you will if you don't give in." Evelyn had nothing to lose and nothing to gain by saying these encouraging words to me. I began to believe in myself just a little bit; maybe I could make something of my life one day and help others in the way Evelyn had said.

One day the doctor came to see me. "John, you're going to another hospital this afternoon for a while. We're sending you to St Vincent's in Fairview. You are not ill enough for this hospital; you will be more comfortable in St Vincent's."

I spent the rest of the morning going around saying goodbye to the patients in the hospital. Some of the "Dozy Dozen" as I called them, were still there and I went to each of them in turn. Billy got a bit upset when he heard I was going.

"Look, Billy, you take care of the place while I am gone, will you?"

"Ok John," Billy sniffled.

"I'll come and s-see you when I am well enough, Billy, OK?"

"Do ye promise, John?"

"I do, Billy."

I then went to say goodbye to Evelyn. She was quite upset when I told her I was going. I gave her a great big hug and left her. We both had tears in our eyes and I couldn't handle that.

Seven o'clock that evening a nurse told me that a taxi was waiting outside to take us to the hospital. I had begun to feel so accepted here that in one sense I was sad to go. On the other hand I was delighted to leave all the pain and abuse behind me. I got my bags and said my final goodbyes. All the patients who were compus mentus enough came to the big locked door to say goodbye to me. To my surprise Evelyn was standing at the door when it opened.

"Bye, everyone," I shouted as I turned to go. I could see Billy in the background looking very sad, his long black hair hanging and his posture one of hopelessness and hurt.

"See ya, Billy," I shouted. "Take care of things h-here for me, will you?" He looked up and gave a little smile and a defeated wave of his hand. I turned to say goodbye to Evelyn. She was in tears. She hugged me affectionately and sobbed as she said, "Stay clean, John – you can do it."

I had made some good friends in St Brendan's. I felt more loved by some people in there than I did by people outside.

St Vincent's

The taxi whisked through the quiet evening traffic of Dublin to St Vincent's Psychiatric Hospital in Fairview. The first evening that I was there they gave me my usual medication. I slept in St Theresa's Ward. This hospital was a little cleaner than St Brendan's was but some of the patients were in a pretty bad state. Like at St Brendan's, some of them had lived in the hospital for twenty years or more. The morning after my arrival the doctor saw me and told me that I would be coming off my barbiturates and Valium.

"I have decided to give you Meloril. They will relax you and you will be fine."

I argued with the doctor, telling him that I did not feel ready to come off the barbiturates or Valium.

"I am not fully w-withdrawn yet and this drug Meloril that you want to g-give me is not in the same family of medicines."

I knew a little about medication and tried to convince the doctor that I was not ready to come off Benzodiazepines. He wouldn't listen to me. I was not ready for this and I in no way felt ready to come off all other medication. The decision had been made, however, and I had no choice in the matter. At medication time that day I was given Meloril and I began to withdraw from the other medication. I was very sick when my mother came up to see me that evening. She was upset.

"John," she said, "I didn't know that you were using the needle and injecting yourself. I just found out from St Brendan's that your arms were in a terrible state when you went in there. Your uncle works there and he has told us how sick you were and how addicted you were."

"Ma, they had no business telling you that. Anything that happens to me in St Brendan's or any medication I was on is private and confidential." I was really angry with them for giving my mother this private information. The new medication I was on was having a terrible effect on me. My mouth was drying up and my head was throbbing. My brain was going faster than I could keep up with. When I tried to talk, my thoughts came quicker than my mouth could speak. I was stuttering worse than ever. Some friends came to see me and I could tell that my conversation made no sense to them. I caught them taking a sidewards glance at each other that said, "John's lost the plot this time; let's get out of here." I tried to explain to them what was wrong but the words would not come out the way I wanted them to. My friends did not visit me again during my stay in St Vincent's.

I pleaded with the doctor on a daily basis to take me off this terrible medication but he wouldn't. My mind was in torment, racing, racing, racing; it just wouldn't slow down. After over a week of this I slipped out of the hospital and ran to a doctor's surgery where I knew I could get Valium. The surgery was only about a half-mile away. Within half-an-hour I had two weeks supply of 5mg Valium. I took about 30 of them in one go, chewing them up and swallowing them. Twenty minutes later I was feeling normal again; it was such a relief. That Meloril was really cracking me up.

I stayed in the hospital for about another week. I had to take part in the ridiculous disco and exercise lessons every day. Every time I got the Meloril I would hold it under my tongue and spit it out into my hand as soon as I was around the corner, and then throw it into a bin. I managed to get medication and alcohol for myself from outside doctors and chemists and local off-licences for the remainder of my stay in St Vincent's. I felt so sorry for the patients there; some of them were very sick and many of them were getting electric shock treatment. They would go out for the treatment feeling very nervous and come back about an hour later like zombies. I never saw it do any of them any good.

I left the hospital after staying as long as I could. I came home to our house and made promises once again to my family that I would get my life together. I didn't tell them that I was already addicted to Valium again.

I did not know it then, but I would visit St Brendan's, St Vincent's and other mental hospitals and detox centres at least another ten times and have similar experiences in the years that followed.

Chapter Twelve
A Geographical Change

Portugal

My dad thought that maybe a geographical change would do the trick: get me away to a different climate, different culture and give me a chance to get my act together and no doubt create a bit of peace at home as well. He phoned my sister Pauline in Portugal and asked if I could go and stay with her for a while. She agreed, so long as I did not cause any trouble. She and her husband Cesar had two children now, Peter and Pilar. They were lovely children and I relished the idea of spending time with my niece and nephew. Within one week my dad had it all arranged. Pauline worked in the Irish Embassy in Portugal; Cesar worked in the bank. They had two maids to look after all the cooking and cleaning. I couldn't wait to go.

I flew out and was met at Lisbon airport by Pauline, Cesar, and the two children. They took me to their beautiful apartment down on the coast in Oeiras near Lisbon. I was thrilled to be there with them all. I had secretly brought a week's supply of drugs with me to keep me going till I got to know the scene over there. Pauline had organised a job for me in a hairdresser's owned by a friend of hers near the Ritz Hotel in Lisbon. This job was only intended to help me get back on my feet, so I didn't receive a wage. I did, however, get some good tips. It was arranged for me to work there for two or three days a week. Within days I knew where to get drugs on the streets of Lisbon and they were quite cheap compared to Dublin. A bottle of wine cost the equivalent of eleven pence and a pack of 25 cigarettes was only the equivalent of eighteen pence. Most days when I wasn't working I armed myself with fags, drugs and booze and headed off to the beach. This was the life: sun, sea, sand and cheap booze, fags and drugs. I thought for a while that I was in heaven. The two maids at Pauline's house did everything for me – they even ironed my socks! I couldn't believe it. Unfortunately it was not long before problems began to arise.

I was down by the beach one day with an addict I had got to know and I invited him home to my sister's house to drink a couple of bottles of wine with me. Obviously my behaviour patterns had not changed and now the honeymoon period with my sister's family was coming to an end. I had managed to cut down on the Valium by using other drugs, so I had convinced myself that I was doing well. We drank a lot of wine at my sister's that day. I must have fallen into a drunken sleep because the next thing I can remember was my sister standing over me shouting and screaming. She had come home to find the front door open and all her jewellery gone from the house. It was not very expensive jewellery but it was of great sentimental value. Cesar came home then and he lost the plot altogether. They did not believe my story that I had invited a Portuguese guy to the house and he had stolen the stuff; they insisted that I had sold the jewellery. The whole family was upset. Peter and Pilar were both too young to understand what was going on. Once again I felt a terrible sense of failure. I had let everyone down and I felt absolutely ashamed of myself. They were very angry for some days but they gave me one last chance to sort myself out.

I managed to pull myself together for a while and some trust was given back to me. The Irish Ambassador's son was due to take a holiday in Portugal and I was asked to show him around Lisbon. I had every intention of taking good care of him and giving him a day to remember. I picked him up from the main train station in Lisbon, but not before I had bought some drugs to give me the confidence to take care of him for the day. I was nervous. I had promised myself that I would not get drunk or stoned. The trouble is, an active addict and alcoholic can never make promises to himself or others and be sure of keeping them. That is the selfishness of addiction.

A GEOGRAPHICAL CHANGE

"You must be John," he said as he arrived at our pre-arranged meeting place just outside the railway station.

"Yes I am, and you're Martin," I replied. He was a pretty ordinary-looking guy and it turned out that he and his family only lived a half-mile from our house in Dublin.

"Hey, do ye fancy a drink before I give you a tour of the city?"

"Sure," he replied. "Where to?"

"There's a great bar just around the corner here – we'll go in there."

We stayed there for a couple of hours and I was knocking back the booze and pills. I then took a complete blackout; I do not remember any of the rest of the day. I am told that I brought him out to Estoril, a lovely holiday area about 25 miles from Lisbon. I continued to drink and take pills. It was Martin who ended up taking me home to my sister's house. He had to phone the Irish Embassy to find out from his father, the Ambassador, where I lived. I was so drunk and stoned that Pauline could not even talk to me when Martin brought me home. She was totally embarrassed and very angry with me. The next day she told me to pack my bags and get out of the house.

"Where will I go?" I argued.

"I don't know and I don't care," Pauline said. Cesar was understandably very angry also; he helped me to pack my bags. My other sister Geraldine was visiting Pauline at this time and she gave me some money to help me on my way.

I left Pauline's house with a few hundred escudos in my pocket. I was in a strange country; my family didn't want to know me; I was still feeling sick from my escapade the day before and I was feeling very lonely and depressed. I wished once again that I had never been born. Yet something inside me wouldn't let me give in. "One day everything will be all right" – I somehow knew that.

I went into a market in Lisbon and bought myself an ex-army sleeping bag. It had arms in it. I bought a dagger to protect myself with and to open cans of beans and other food items. I also bought a cheap bottle to hold water or wine. That day I filled it with wine.

I phoned Pauline to let her know that I was OK and that I intended to hitchhike home. She was relieved to hear my voice and she told me to be careful.

"I will," I promised. "Tell Cesar I'm sorry and thanks for everything and tell the kids I love them." I was crying now so I hung up the phone.

Dicing with Death

I got the bus to the outskirts of Lisbon and tried to hitch a lift. I was on a dual carriageway that was well lit. I waited for ages but no lift came. There was a wood behind me so I decided to go in among the trees and sleep there for the night. I walked about twenty yards into the wood; it was dry there and the ground was soft with fallen pine needles. I laid out my Portuguese army sleeping bag, put my haversack down as a pillow and climbed into my bed for the night. I noticed that there was a zip that I could undo to let my feet out if I needed to. I put my knife under my haversack/pillow and lay down. I couldn't sleep; the last few days' events were going through my head and I had a strong sense of failure, guilt and shame. I looked up through the trees at the stars.

"God," I cried, "why am I like I am? I cannot seem to take charge of my life and I'm hurting everyone that I care for."

I must have lain there for about half an hour when suddenly I heard a horrible growling sound behind me; then another one and another. My heart began to pound. I chanced a glance behind me and to my horror I could see five or six big dogs. They looked like wild dogs. I reached behind my head and took out my dagger. Then I reached down quickly but carefully and unzipped the foot of the sleeping bag. I then pushed my legs out. I had left my boots on so all I had to do now was grab my haversack, take the knife in my hand, jump up and run for my life. The dogs were getting nearer now and they were becoming bolder; the growling was louder and more vicious. I could almost feel their foul breath on my neck as I jumped up, grabbed my bag and ran. In an instant the dogs were after me, barking and growling. One of them jumped at me. I could feel his paws on my back and legs as he lunged. I held the dagger in my right hand and swung it back with force again and again. I could hear a squeal as the blade hit its mark. I was within a few yards of the road now; I could see the lights clearly through the trees. Another dog jumped at me and nipped the back of my right leg. I swung the dagger blindly behind me, trying desperately to keep the dogs away from me. Suddenly I broke through the trees and rushed out onto the well-lit but lonely road. I ran to the middle of the road and turned round quickly. I put my left arm out in front of me, at the same time holding the dagger firmly in my right hand to fight the dogs off with. Amazingly they had not followed me. They stayed skulking by the trees for a while and then they retreated back into the woods. Suddenly I remembered something that one of the doctors had said to me when I was beaten up, and the thought crossed my mind: "Somebody up there is looking after me." I looked up at the starry sky for a second; then shrugged my shoulders and said to myself, "Don't be daft." I took out my supply of wine and swallowed the lot. Then I quickly made my way back into Lisbon and slept in the bus station for the night.

The next day I filled my wine bottle again but I also drank two bottles before I left on the bus. I ended up falling asleep on the back seat of the bus. When I awoke I vomited everywhere. The bus driver stopped the bus and made me get off. I knew I was somewhere between Lisbon and the Spanish–Portuguese border. I hitched the rest of the way and got several lifts. When I finally made it into Spain it was very hot, probably over 100 degrees. I continued hitching and eventually a young guy stopped and brought me all the way to Madrid. I bought some French-style bread to eat and a cheap bottle of wine to wash it down. That night I slept in a bush under a tree near Real Madrid's football ground. The next morning I went to the Irish Consulate and asked them to help me. My family back in Ireland would not buy me a ticket home. My dad's philosophy now was, "John got himself into this mess so let him get himself out." I phoned my Auntie Eileen free from the Irish Consulate and she agreed to pay my fare on the train. It would take a few days to sort it out, but in the meantime the Irish Consulate agreed to put me up in a B&B. They also agreed to give me a small sum of money every day. It wasn't much; I had to be careful with it. I was withdrawing from all the wine I had been drinking so I rationed myself a little Anise, every day; not enough to get drunk but enough to keep me sane. I bought cans of beans, which I opened, with my knife. I survived in this way.

The train journey home was uneventful: Madrid to Paris, Paris to Calais, Calais to Dover on the ferry; then the train to London, London to Holyhead, the ferry to Dublin and home. It took three-and-a-half days to complete the journey. I couldn't face going home to my parents' house so I went and stayed with a friend of mine in Rathmines, Dublin. He was a drug addict and a drinker as well. I got absolutely stoned out of my mind the first day home, so much so that I woke up the next day and found I had lost a four false-teeth plate. I looked everywhere for them but they were nowhere to be found. My mate told me that I had been sick the night before and had probably vomited them down the toilet. At all events they were gone.

When I finally went home I looked a mess. I had a tan from being in Lisbon and from hitching in the hot weather, but my skin was all blotchy and now my teeth were missing. My family were not happy to see me; they didn't say much to me but I could tell that the fight had gone out of them. I was glad in one sense, as I could not handle another row with my father. There was no free dental care in Ireland at that time so I improvised by using an old set of my dad's falsers. I measured the gap in my own teeth and with a hacksaw I cut my dad's old teeth down to fit my mouth. I had to file bits off here and there before I could get them to fit in. By the time I was finished I looked like Ken Dodd. No matter what I did, the teeth stuck out. I didn't care; all feelings of self-worth and self-respect were gone.

Chapter Thirteen
Drugs, Drink, Death and Doss-houses

The Valley of the Shadow of Death

My mam came into my room to speak to me; she sat me down on the bed and to my surprise she gave me one of those great big ma hugs. I hung on to her. I loved her so much and I loved my family but I just couldn't seem to stop hurting them. My ma held my two shoulders in her hands and pushed me forward a bit so that she could look at me. By the expression on her face I could tell that she was about to tell me something serious.

"John, two of your pals died while you were away; one from a drug overdose and the other from a swimming accident while he was drunk. We were afraid to tell you while you were with Pauline, in case it set you off again. I'm so sorry, John. If you don't do something about your life you could be next."

I knew this could be true but no alcoholic or addict thinks that they will be killed by their addiction. A weird kind of belief that you are invincible takes over. *Others might die but not me*. I had been sick, though, with hepatitis, pleurisy, and some kind of blood-poisoning that made me very ill and caused me to break out in septic sores all over my body. I had lost count of the guys who had died in our area. Several from our gang were now dead. Going to funerals had become a sick excuse to get stoned down at the bus shelter and drink a toast to their memory. Secretly we all wondered who would be next.

The police were regular callers to our bus shelter now. Most of us, including me, had spent many weekends in the cells down at Clontarf police station. Our friendships were falling apart and some of the guys were finding it hard to cope with their withdrawals and addiction.

One evening I was having a drink with a couple of my close pals in a local pub. It was still early so there were not many in the lounge. One couple were playing pool while some other people were chatting in a corner. Suddenly Tim changed the direction of the conversation in such a way that it startled me slightly. He asked us, "How much cyanide would it take to kill an elephant?" The talk continued along those lines until we debated how much it would take to kill a man. We drank on for a few hours and then made our way home.

The next morning I got a phone call from a friend, Johnny. "I've got some bad news for you," he said. "Tim is dead. He was found in his armchair this morning. They think he has taken cyanide."

That funeral was particularly difficult. Tim was one of the pillars of our gang. He had more sense than the rest of us; he held down a job, owned his own house and had a beautiful wife and child. Now he was dead.

Shortly afterwards another friend and neighbour jumped from a bridge in front of a train. His body was mashed all over the tracks. He too left a lovely girlfriend and baby. He was another one who seemed more together than I was, or so I had thought. What was happening?

Not long after that I was in a pub in Baggot Street with some of the lads. I was now back using barbiturates: Diconal, Palfium, speed, whatever I could get my hands on. One of my friends went to get the last bus home. I left shortly after him thinking I would see him at the bus stop, but he was not there. I called to his house the next day but he was not there either. Three days later his body was found in the River Liffey. This was one of my closest friends and he was now dead. I could not take it any more. I decided to get out of Ireland and make a fresh start somewhere. I could not go to his funeral and listen to the priest saying things like "Even though I walk through the valley of the shadow of death I will fear no evil." The truth was I was getting frightened; my life was completely out of control.

"Shine On, You Crazy Diamond"

My mind was in great turmoil; I was completely confused, I had no sense of direction, there was no one around to speak to who understood me. Indeed I couldn't even understand myself. I didn't know who I was or who I was meant to be. I was a mixed-up assortment of nice, admirable things that I saw in others, but I was also full of my own anger, guilt, shame and confusion. I was desperate to get peace into my mind and it was critical to me that I made some kind of progress; life had to go on. There was no giving in; suicide was not an option to me. I would press on and get my life together – somehow, sometime.

During this particularly depressing time of my life I listened a lot to an album called *Wish You Were Here* by Pink Floyd. I listened to the words of one of the songs in particular:

Remember when you were young, you shone like the sun,
* Shine on, you crazy diamond.*
Now there's a look in your eyes, like black holes in the sky.
* Shine on, you crazy diamond.*
Come on you target for far away laughter, come on you
* stranger, you legend, you martyr, and shine!*
Come on you raver, you seer of visions, come on you
* painter, you piper, you prisoner, and Shine.*

I felt like a crazy diamond, like there was a lot of good inside me waiting to get out. There was also a lot of craziness in me and this had to go somehow. I would shine one day, I would make it one day, I would not give in, I had to make it; I owed it to myself and to my family. I deserved better.

One day I asked my ma for a few quid to help me get over to London.

"Ma," I said, "I need to get out of here. Everyone is dying; I can't handle it any more."

She gave me just enough to get over there. I packed a small bag that night and didn't say goodbye to anyone except my family. The next morning I got up early and headed for Dun Laoghaire port on the south side of Dublin for the boat to Holyhead in North Wales; from there I got the train to Euston

Station in London. I was reasonably familiar with London, having made a couple of brief visits there before, so I headed to the West End just to get something to sort myself out. I was feeling very vulnerable.

I got the Tube train from Euston Station to Piccadilly Circus in London's West End. I knew that I could get some drugs at Platform Four, so I headed through the crowds of people and eventually came out there. Sure enough, there was someone selling Tuinal barbiturates, 3 grain; five for a pound.

"Great; I'm sorted. Where will I get a 'works' around here?" I asked the guy.

"Up in the 24-hour chemist on Shaftesbury Avenue," he answered.

I headed straight for the chemist shop. There were lots of addicts hanging around Shaftesbury Avenue. They were a sick-looking lot, gaunt and thin, the walking dead. I went into the chemist's and asked if they had any syringes and needles. I felt very self-conscious asking for them; this was a new experience for me. Free clean needles.

"How many do you want?" the shop assistant asked me.

"Just one, please." I took it and left.

I headed back down to Piccadilly Circus and went into the toilets to have a hit. There were so many people in there that I couldn't use the taps at the basins to get clean water. Instead I went into a cubical and flushed the toilet, filling the syringe with enough water to dissolve the barbiturate. I then slipped the needle into a vein in my leg and pushed the drug in. "Peace at last" was the final thing I remember saying to myself. The next thing I knew I woke up on the floor of the toilet, the needle still in my leg. I made a quick check to ensure that there was no clotted blood in it. Satisfied that there was none I pushed the rest in and went off again into a semi-coma.

I eventually came to and staggered out of the toilet. Everyone was staring at me. I, too, now looked like one of the walking dead. I made my way down to the Charing Cross Road and found a doorway to sleep in. Someone came along and gave me a blanket and a cup of tea. The next morning I was awakened by the noise of the traffic going past. My head was pounding and my whole body was aching.

"Man," I thought, "I've got off to a bad start here in London. The streets are not paved with gold after all." I decided to try harder that day to get things sorted. Some charity guy came up and gave me a cup of tea and a sandwich. He said to me, "Jesus loves you" and tried to engage me in conversation.

"I'm not able for conversation at the moment," I told him.

"OK," he said. "Have a nice day – I'll be praying for you." He moved on to the next doorway. I could hear him saying, "Here's a cup of tea and a sandwich; Jesus loves you" to the person lying there.

"Nutter," I said to myself. Then I thought, "I have some cheek calling him a nutter and me in the state I'm in. God couldn't love me anyway, not after all I have done. He's finished with me."

I checked my pockets to see how much money I had. There was just over a pound and two Tuinal. I took one of the Tuinal and swallowed it.

"I'll keep the other for later," I thought, "and I'll try to find out about work. You're meant to be getting things together over here, Johnny Edwards, not getting worse. Pull yourself together. *'Shine on you crazy diamond'*."

I knew that I didn't have enough money to get by and I had no way of getting it, not unless I begged for it.

"Naw," I said aloud; "I couldn't do that. Me, beg for money!" I walked up and down between Charing Cross Road and Trafalgar Square, trying to figure out how I could get some money without begging. I passed many people who were begging; most of them were in their twenties like me. The thought struck me, "Why not give it a try?" By the time I had walked from Trafalgar Square to Piccadilly Circus the Tuinal I had swallowed had taken effect and I felt a level of Dutch courage inside me.

"'Scuse m-me sir, could you s-spare a few p-pence for something to eat?" I stuttered out to a passing workman.

"Piss off, and get yourself a job, you waster," was his reply. A little further up the road I tried again. This time I put a real sad face on and made myself walk with a slight limp. I chose a sympathetic-looking middle-aged woman.

"'Scuse me, Mrs, I'm not h-having much luck finding work at the moment and I'm starving with the hunger; could you help me out with a few pence towards something to eat?" She looked me up and down as if checking for outward signs to tell her whether to say "Yeah" or "Nay" to my request. She put her hand into her handbag and took her purse out. She seemed to take ages. I was embarrassed and was shuffling nervously from foot to foot, holding my head down. I felt the whole world was watching me. Finally she took out a pound note and gave it to me.

"Don't spend it on drink now," she said.

"I won't," I promised. "Thanks very much your kindness," I said to her. She put a little smile on her face and wished me well. It was nice to talk to someone friendly and very nice to have another pound in my pocket. I went straight up to Platform Four and got five more barbiturates, just in case I needed them later. I didn't want to be sick, now, did I?

I spent the rest of the morning begging and made enough to do me for the day. I bought another syringe from the chemist on Shaftesbury Avenue. Then I headed out to the Irish part of town to look for work. I had heard that if I was to go to Cricklewood or Kilburn I might get a job with a subcontractor on a building site. I took the Tube over and went from pub to pub looking for work.

"Wait outside the Crown Pub in Cricklewood at seven in the morning and you will get work," I was told.

"Great," I thought. "Now all I have to do is find somewhere to stay." I asked some of the Irish navvies where I could find a hostel or some other kind of overnight accommodation.

"There's a place down in Willesden; it's called Willesden Reception Centre, or some people call it the Spike. It's only a short bus ride from here. You'd better hurry, though, if you want to stay there, because they stop taking people in at about four o'clock."

"OK, thanks," I said as I left the pub. I got the bus down to the centre, taking one more Tuinal on the way. It took me a little while to find the place. It was situated next to a Jewish graveyard. By the time I arrived, the Tuinal had taken effect. I was now stoned, quite stoned, because I had been drinking in the pubs looking for work.

I walked down the narrow pathway towards the imposing Victorian house, making a conscious effort to walk straight. There were three or four men standing outside waiting to get in to the centre for the night. After about fifteen minutes a man came out and said that the place was full; there were no rooms available. The other men in the queue just turned on their heels and slowly walked back down the narrow pathway.

"I'm going to the off-licence," one of them said. "I've enough for a can of special brew." They all headed off together. They were a sad-looking bunch of guys, in long coats, and beards. I could tell that they had long given up hope of ever amounting to much in life.

"Do you want to come with us, young 'un?" they asked me.

"OK, thanks," I said and followed. I wasn't sure how to talk to these men, or if they could be trusted. As we walked a black man approached us in the opposite direction. He had some leaflets in his hand.

"Here you are, boys," he said. "There's a Christian tent meeting on up in Willesden Park next week." He gave me a leaflet containing the details of the meeting. I took it and put it in my pocket next to my Tuinal. The black guy talked to us for a while. He was really nice, and he told us that our lives could be changed if we put our trust in God. The other men began to mock and make fun of him. I had listened, though.

"Maybe God is real," I thought. Memories of the "Children of God" in Dublin came back to me. They were weird but they were happy.

"Come on, Johnny," one of my new friends shouted to me. "Are you coming with us?" We continued on down the road. I had my money stuck down my sock, so that was safe.

"Don't worry, Johnny," he said. "We won't bite you. You're one of us now. You'll be all right with us." We walked on down the road to the off-licence and between us we bought a few cans. They filled me in on places where I could stay for free and told me how to get emergency money from the Department of Health and Social Security. We had a good laugh.

I must have had a drug-and-drink-induced blackout then, because the next thing I remember is that I was in a pub; I can't even recall where it was. This English guy was promising me work in the following morning. He even offered to put me up for the night. He then brought me home to his place and gave me some drink. I blacked out again. Next thing I remember is I was sitting on the floor of a shower with water pouring down on me. I was naked and so was he. He was beginning to dress and he said we were going for a drink. I got dried and dressed. I was sore inside myself but I was still so stoned that I couldn't figure out why. He took me down to some part of London where there was a late pub open. He bought me a half-pint of bitter and said, "I'm going to the toilet. I'll be back in a few minutes."

I waited for about a half-an-hour but he never came back. I put my hand in my pocket to check that my Tuinal were still there. They were gone and so was my money. I had nothing left, except that bit of paper about the Christian meeting in Willesden next Saturday. I got up from the stool I was sitting on. I was still very sore inside myself. The truth hit me like a truck: *he had raped me, that bastard; he had sexually abused me.* The horror of it gripped me. I couldn't handle the truth of it, so just as quickly I pushed the thought back down and denied it. I knew it had happened but I wouldn't face up to the reality of it for over ten years.

I walked out into the cold, lonely streets of London. It was about three in the morning; I had no money and nowhere to go. I had been raped and I felt so frightened in this big city that was full of strangers. I walked for hours. The cold was so intense I could feel it all the way through to my bones and I had nowhere to sleep. Eventually a new day dawned and people began to walk about again. I found myself passing a Catholic rectory and decided to call in and ask if one of the priests would give me some money. I mostly just wanted someone to talk to. A priest answered the door, took one look at me and told me that they did not give money out. He then closed the door. I continued walking until I reached the West End of

London again. This was territory I could survive in. I was now in withdrawal; I was completely nervous, very frightened and felt that if I didn't get some drugs inside me soon I would take a fit. I was too nervous and sick to beg, so I asked one of the dealers on Platform Four if he could sort me out with some Tuinal till later.

"I'll tell you what," he said. "The police have been around a few times recently. They're mixing with us by dressing in plain clothes. I'll do a deal with you. If I wait in a café on Dean Street, you go and find a few people who want to score drugs and bring them to me. If you do that I'll sort you out with something for yourself and maybe give you a few bob as well. Deal?"

"Deal," I answered. He showed me the café on Dean Street, near Soho Square. I got busy and it didn't take me long to find a few people who wanted to score drugs: methadone amps, Tuinal, heroin, Ritalin. This dealer had the lot. I brought the "clients" back to an appointed spot near the café, then went and gave him the order.

"Well done," he said. "I'll sort you out after I give them theirs." He was true to his word. He soon returned and gave me five Seconal barbiturates and a couple of amps of Methadone. He also gave me some money. I took two Secanol immediately and started to head down town.

"Hey – are you not going to get me more customers, Paddy?" he shouted after me.

"No, not today," I replied.

"OK. Maybe I'll see you tomorrow on Platform Four?"

"Maybe," I answered and continued on my way. I went into an off-licence and got a couple of cans of special brew with the money; I would eat later when I felt better. I then went into a park just off Shaftesbury Avenue and sat down on one of the benches to wait for the drug to "come on" and to drink my cans. Thoughts of the night before and what that guy had done to me kept rising to the surface. "Even the Catholic priest wouldn't help me," I recalled. I wrestled with these thoughts until somehow I won over them and buried them deep in my subconscious. I would never talk or think about it again, I promised myself. I held myself together pretty well that night and got a place to stay in Dean Street Reception Centre. I still had a few barbs left and the two amps of methadone. I stashed these in some bushes before going into the Dean Street Spike. This was a horrible place; the scum of the earth lived in here; addicts, alcoholics, tramps, down-and-outs, the lot. You even got deloused on the way in if they suspected you might have fleas. I remembered the words of the guy down in Willesden, "You're one of us now, Johnny," he had said. I was one of them, but one day – one day I would get out of it. Maybe I'd win the Irish Sweeps or something like that.

That night I shared a big dormitory with about twenty other men. The place was full of the stink of dirty socks, sweat, old clothes and stale booze breath. It was obnoxious. The bed linen itself was clean but I felt soiled just by being in that place. I was tired and decided to go to bed early. I went to use the toilet before going to bed. I pushed the cubical door open and inside I discovered a guy having a fix in his groin. I could actually see the gaping black hole in his groin that he was groping around in trying to find the vein. He looked at me; then stood up with his trousers down around his ankles and, pointing the syringe at me, he said he would infect me with hepatitis B if I didn't get out of the cubical. I didn't argue; I went immediately into a different cubical and then went to bed. I slept the whole night through. Next morning we had to clean the place, mop the floors and sweep the stairs. I was feeling very sick and couldn't wait to get down to my stash of drugs. They seemed to keep us for ages. I had to get out but they wouldn't let us go until the work was finished. The next thing I knew I was lying on the floor with people looking down at me.

"Are you OK?" they asked.

"Yea," I answered. "Why?" My head felt like a huge electric shock had gone through it.

"You've taken some kind of fit, John," one of the staff told me. "You'd better stay in here for a while before you go out."

"No, honest, I'll be fine – I just need to get some fresh air." I staggered to my feet and made my way to the front door. I stumbled down Dean Street with one thing in mind, I had to get my barbs as quickly as I could.

DRUGS, DRINK, DEATH AND DOSS-

I made it down to the park without taking another fit and retrieved my stash of drugs from under the bush where I had hidden them. "Oh, thank God they're still here; I don't know what I would have done if they were gone . . ." I quickly put three in my mouth and swallowed them. They weren't as strong as the 3 grain Tuinal but they were easily strong enough to sort me out. Once the drugs began to take effect I went out begging for some money. I remember I made eighteen pounds that day, a lot of money in 1979. Later that same day, in a toilet, I tried the methadone amps, shooting it straight into a vein in my arm. It had a completely different effect from barbs and I really liked it. I was more in control taking this.

I managed to get myself into the Willesden Reception Centre that night. This was a lot cleaner than the other hostel: everyone had to have a shower on the way in. The first night I was in there they deloused me with a horrible white powder that stunk to high heaven; then they gave me a white gown to wear while my clothes were being deloused. I saw a man examine the neck of my jumper under a light to see if my clothes had lice on them. I had to walk into the dining area wearing the white gown, and even the down-and-outs in there backed off me when they smelt the white powder and saw the gown I was in.

"Now even the tramps of the world are rejecting me," I thought wryly. I was high on methadone and didn't mind so much. I had a stash of drugs outside the place for the following day, but I took the trouble to smuggle in one Tuinal for the morning, to make sure I didn't take any fits.

I had lost the piece of paper giving the details of the Christian meeting in the park on Saturday night. When Saturday came I drank a bottle of cheap sherry and had a cocktail of drugs. In the evening I remembered about the meeting. I made my way up to the park and there I could see the tent, full of people praising God. It was good; I enjoyed watching it. Then some guy preached and at the end of his talk he gave an invitation to come forward and give your life to God and be baptised. There was a big, round pool on the stage that people were going to be baptised in. I was standing at the open door of the big tent, very stoned and drunk but with something inside me wanting to go up. I marched boldly to the front, staggering a few times on the way. Some people managed to beat me to it. They climbed the steps in front of me and stood at the edge of the stage by the pool. Some of them were dressed in white gowns for some reason. I was in my dirty jeans and an old worn jacket. I stood there for ages. The preacher prayed with, and baptised, all the people in front of me, one by one, and even the ones behind me in the queue. Eventually I was left standing on my own. I was beginning to feel stupid and very embarrassed. The preacher kept talking and completely ignored me. *Maybe God didn't want me*, I thought; *maybe I was not good enough.* I looked across the big tent to the door that I had come in through. It looked like it was 100 yards away, although in reality it was only about 40 feet. I made a decision to make my way out again. I felt so stupid walking back down the steps again, and to make it worse I had to walk diagonally across the tent in front of everyone to get back out. No one came to talk to me; they didn't even look at me – it was like I didn't exist. In one way I was glad but in another I was feeling very hurt. It seemed to me that even the Christians don't want to know me.

"Oh boy!" It had been a tough few days. I began to cry bitter tears as I walked down the road. That night I slept rough under layers of plastic paper at the back of the bus station near the Spike. It was raining and somehow little rivulets of rain managed to course their way down to where I was trying to sleep and to drip on top of me and down my neck. I eventually had to move. I found a garage door open down an alley. The garage was empty; I lay on the cold concrete floor and slept fitfully for a while. By the time morning arrived I was beginning to go into hypothermia; I was cold to the core.

My life continued in a vicious circle of drug and drink abuse for about another year. I was in and out of different hostels and spikes. Often I slept on the streets down London's West End, begging to exist. I sometimes managed to get some work on building sites and factories, but I was on a downward spiral, with my life spinning out of control. Yet I managed to find ways to survive even when there was no work. Nuns down by the Grand Union Canal would give me soup and dry bread; or a girl in the local chipper would give me her lunch of chicken and chips sometimes. I was, by now, losing weight and getting quite sick. The fits were becoming more regular.

"Sally Army"

In winter time, after spending the night on the streets, I would get on the Circle Line Tube train when it started at about five-thirty in the morning and just travel round in circles. This way I kept warm and could have a sleep. One particular morning I got off the train and made my way down Ladbroke Grove to Portobello Market. I sometimes went down there to get fruit from the market stall vendors. If there was fruit that was beginning to go rotten or that had a bad bit in it they would throw it in a box at the back of their pitches near the footpath. I would come along and pick it up and eat it. There was also a Salvation Army hall down there that gave food out free of charge. This particular day I picked up my fruit and then begged enough money for a few cans of special brew. I had plenty of barbiturates or methadone those days, as I had managed to find several doctors who would give me a prescription for basically anything I wanted. One of these doctors was practising in Willesden; he had given me a prescription for 90 Tuinal for the price of a bottle of whisky a few days before. I was completely addicted to them. I now had long hair and my weight was down to between seven and eight stone.

I got some half-decent pears and apples from the back of one of the vendors' patches. I walked a bit and sat down on the edge of the road near the "Sally Army" hall to eat the fruit. While I ate I began to think about my life and the way it was still going downhill. I was becoming more anxious about it; lately I had begun to do things that I really didn't want to do. Sometimes I ate out of bins. If I saw someone throw half a hamburger or a good sandwich into a bin I would take the food out when I thought nobody was looking and eat it. I hardly ever bought cigarettes any more; instead I would pick up dog ends, tear them open and roll them up before smoking them. Sometimes I would walk around the West End of London and Oxford Street late at night before the street sweepers came along and get the day's pickings of dog-ends, often enough to fill a 2 oz. tin with. I had also taken to drinking Jack, which is a mixture of surgical spirits and water. It had a disgusting taste and, as we say in Dublin, it would take the brass off a brass monkey. On two occasions I vomited up the lining of my stomach. Pints of blood came up with it; yet it never stopped me drinking or taking drugs. I guess I was lucky I didn't die or haemorrhage.

I had got particularly concerned when one day a group of Scottish punks and I decided to mug someone in Green Park. It was in the early evening, between twilight and darkness. The lighting from the streets didn't penetrate far into the park. People taking a short cut through the park had to cross a little bridge; they would go quickly across this bridge and hurry on until they came into the light and safety at the other side of the park. At this time of night you always had some people taking a chance before it got really dark. It was one of those risk-takers that we would target. We had it all planned out. We would hide behind a few trees just on the other side of the bridge. As soon as a suitable mugging candidate came along – someone not too big and not too old, in case he died of fright – we would surprise him, hit him and push him to the ground, take his wallet and run away in different directions, meeting later in Trafalgar Square.

When the time came, my friends hid behind some trees down near the lake. We waited for some poor and innocent passer-by that looked like he might have some money on him. I could see a businessman approaching us in the distance. He seemed to be in his late-50s or thereabouts; he didn't look too fit.

"Here's our man, lads," I said. They began to get excited; the adrenalin was running high but they were making too much noise. The victim was getting nearer and I was sure he would hear us.

"For crying out loud, will ye be quiet, lads!" I whispered sharply. "He's getting near. If you don't shut up he'll hear us and run away. Stay hidden, now. Nobody move until I give a signal." Some of the other guys had done this before. They were Scottish lads, punk rockers, sporting blue, pink or green Mohican hairstyles, with safety pins and chains attached to their clothes and all of them glue-sniffers. I could hear one of them take a few gulps of glue vapour from one of the glue-filled plastic bags that they always seemed to carry around with them. Then the sickly smell of glue wafted past me.

"Oh, for God's sake," I said to myself, "I must be completely mad to be doing this." But it was too late to stop now; the guy was only about ten yards away from us, then five, four, three . . .

"NOW!" I shouted and ran out in front of the man. He was a West Indian; his eyes bulged and he let out a terrified gasp as he saw these Mohicans led by a skinny guy with an Irish accent descend on him. I hit him on the side of his head with my fist and he went down like a sack of potatoes. The other lads gathered around, getting ready to hit him again. One of them gave him a couple of kicks in his ribs and said, "Give us your wallet."

"Leave him alone," I said. "I have his wallet." I had taken it out of the inside left pocket of his jacket. Another one of the lads kicked him again.

"Leave him alone!" I shouted. I was kneeling on his chest with one knee against his neck. I had made the mistake of looking at his face. He was absolutely terrified and he was crying. Our eyes met and there was a plea for mercy in them. It was as if he recognised compassion or some kind of goodness in me, that this was not my normal behaviour. In an instant my life flashed before me and I knew I was not brought up to do this kind of thing. I couldn't go through with it. I looked up at the five punks; all of them were looking at me, waiting for directions.

"Lads," I said, "I'm giving this man back his wallet. What we're doing is wrong. There's no excuse for it and I, for one, am ashamed of myself."

"On ye go, ye mad Paddy!" one of the punks said. "That'll be right – are ye off yer hid or something?" He made as if to take the wallet from me. I stuck the wallet back in the man's inside jacket pocket; then I helped him to his feet and told him to run. One of the punks tried to stop me letting him go but the others stepped in and said, "Just let the poor wee man go – can ye not see that he's half scared to death?"

"Go on, get out of here," I said, "and by the way, we're sorry." You never saw anyone run as fast as that man did through Green Park that night. He must have easily beaten the four-minute mile.

Chapter Fourteen
Helping Hands

Now as I sat by the side of the road in Portobello Market I began to daydream about the man and his family; he had probably gone home that night to a nice warm house.

His wife would have held him when he walked through the front door. One of the kids would have got him a cup of tea, or maybe a drink. He would then have told his family about what had happened. I laughed a little to myself when I imagined him trying to explain the incident. I could see the big home fire blazing up the chimney, his wife sitting on the arm of his armchair bathing his wounds and his kids sitting around on the floor in front of him holding his legs to comfort him . . .

"Well, honey, this skinny little Irish guy and about ten punks with spiky hair – green, blue and red – came running at me from nowhere. They hit me to the ground, kicked me and then took my wallet. Suddenly the Irish guy gave it back to me and told me to get out of here. He had my wallet and he gave it back! The guy must be nuts." I imagined his family being strong around him and loving him. I wished I were in his shoes. I wished that I had a family to encourage me and love me through my trials . . .

"Excuse me."

"Eh, wha'?"

"Excuse me – would you like a cup of tea and a sandwich, son?" I snapped out of my daydreaming and looked around. A woman and man in Salvation Army uniform stood there.

"Come into the hall and we'll give you something to eat, son," they said.

"Thanks – I will," I answered.

They brought me into a room at the back of the hall and made me a lovely sandwich full of ham and salad.

"Do you want salad cream on it, son?" they asked. "What's your name? You haven't told us yet."

"Johnny Edwards – and yes, please, I'd l-love loads of salad cream on the sandwich," I answered. Then they gave me a mug of hot tea to finish off the banquet.

"Well, it's nice to meet you, Johnny. Our names our David and Lorraine Wakefield; we are the captains of this Salvation Army hall."

"We've seen you come into the hall for food on Wednesday nights once or twice over the last few weeks, Johnny. Do you stay around here?"

"Yeah," I answered between bites of the delicious ham sandwich and slurps of hot tea. "I have been down for something to eat a c-couple of times, but I don't l-live around here. I'm staying on the streets up in the West End at the moment."

"That's a shame, Johnny. Can you not get a flat or a hostel to stay in?"

"No, not at the moment; I'm in too much of a mess. I hate staying in some of the hostels anyway; the streets are safer – you get less hassle."

"Oh, I know what you mean. We meet a lot of people from the streets who say that."

"Excuse us a minute Johnny; David and I have to go out to the office for a moment," Lorraine said. "Will you be all right for a couple of minutes?"

"I'll be grand," I answered.

They were back in about five minutes and this time they both sat down at the table with me. Lorraine reached out to take my hand to comfort me, but I pulled mine back from her.

"Johnny," David asked, "do you want to get off the streets and get your life together?"

"You better believe I do," I answered. "But I just can't manage to do it on my own; I need some help."

HELPING HANDS

David then said, "Would you be prepared to go to a rehabilitation centre if we helped you, Johnny?"

"Of course," I said, jumping at the chance. "I'm addicted to barbiturates, though, and Valium. I would n-need a lot of help coming off of them."

"Well, Johnny, here is what we can do for you. We have a couple of spare rooms in our house. You are welcome to use one of them until you get off drugs, but only so long as you go to a rehabilitation centre when you're clean from drugs."

"OK, I'll d-do it," I answered.

"You would not be allowed out on your own, and you would have to help us make up the food for the homeless on Wednesday nights. You would also have to do your bit around the house. OK, Johnny?"

"Sounds great to me," I said. "When can I come to stay with you?"

"Today," they answered.

"Oh!" I said, "I-I wasn't expecting it to be so soon. I have some clothes up in the left luggage department in King's Cross Station – I'd need to get those first." What I was really thinking was that I would need to get some barbs to sort me out for a couple of days.

"OK, Johnny, you go get your things and come down to meet us here later this evening. What time can you meet us, John? Would seven o'clock be OK?"

"Yeah, seven is fine." I calculated that that gave me about four hours to get my things and get some barbs. "Where will I meet you?" I asked them.

"Outside the hall at seven," David said.

"Right then; I'd better be getting a move on if I'm going to get back in time." I finished my tea quickly, and got up to go. "Eh – t-thanks v-very much for helping me. I appreciate it – honest."

"That's OK, Johnny, it's our privilege. Go on, then; get your things and we'll see you later."

"Right – I'll see you then; at seven, right?"

"Yes, seven."

I bolted out of the door and walked up the road with a new spring in my step. Wow! – I was going to stay in a real house tonight, and sleep in a real bed, a clean one – maybe get a bath, and good food. Oh, things were looking good.

I knew this was a chance for me to get things right in my life and I did not want to blow it. I would not get stoned today. I was determined to give this my best effort. I went up to the West End, got my dirty old bag of clothes, five barbs and then I headed back down to Portobello Road. I was going to be early but I didn't want to hang around the West End, as I knew I would probably bump into someone who had drugs or drink. I didn't trust myself not to get caught up in a session and so miss my chance to get my life sorted. When I arrived at Portobello I bought myself a *Daily Mirror*, went into a café, bought a pot of tea and waited the hour and a half until I was to meet David and Lorraine.

My mind began to wander. Now that I was making an effort to get myself sorted, I could afford to think about my family back in Dublin. I hadn't phoned or written to any of them in quite a while. Last time I had written I told my ma and da that I was doing well. I pretended I had a nice flat, a girlfriend and a good job. I loved my family and I didn't want them to know how I was really living. Now I thought, "I'll get myself sorted, go back to Dublin and visit them as soon as I can." I dreamed of walking down our road in Clontarf, Dublin, and up our driveway. My ma would probably see me coming. The front door would open up and she and my da would run down the path to welcome me with a big hug. My whole family would be glad to see me. I snapped out of the dream and realised that I had a smile on my face. Oh! It would be good to go home to see my family and make them proud of me one day.

I read the paper, daydreamed a bit more and then left to meet David and Lorraine. I was fifteen minutes early. I took one barb out of the little brown bottle in my pocket. "That should be enough to hold me for the night," I thought.

"Hi, Johnny," David and Lorraine said as they came round the corner down by the "Sally Army" hall. "We weren't sure if you'd make it back. We were praying that you would."

Here, John, give me your bag and I'll carry it for you; we live not far from here."

HELPING HANDS

David and Lorraine brought me to their home. I was the only person staying with them at that point, although another guy would come a few days later. They showed me my room. It was lovely. The bed was so comfortable, like nothing I had slept in recently; with clean, fresh sheets, the top one folded back over the soft duvet. Two big pillows were placed at the head of the bed and a bedside light sat on a little table next to the bed. There was a big window that had a nice view onto the quiet street below. David then showed me around the house. The bathroom was just beside my room. I couldn't wait to have a bath. I had my own lounge downstairs, and in the basement was the kitchen that was to be used by guests like me.

Lorraine was preparing dinner, so I had a chance to bathe and put some of my clothes in the washing machine. I was very embarrassed when I gave my clothes to David; they were filthy and a bit smelly as well. David took them and said, "Is this all you have Johnny?"

"Yes," I answered, and my face reddened.

"Well, we'll sort out a few things for you tomorrow, OK?"

"Thanks, David," I replied.

"You go and have a bath now; dinner should be ready by the time you've finished."

I had the most relaxing bath, and remained soaking in it for ages. I shaved myself also with a new razor that David gave me. The aroma of food was wafting up the stairs from the kitchen where Lorraine was preparing dinner. Oh! This was good! I had missed these home comforts.

I had to get back into some of my dirty clothes as the others were still being washed. I then went downstairs for dinner. Lorraine had cooked roast lamb, roast spuds, ordinary spuds, peas and gravy – after which we had trifle (non-alcoholic). I can still remember the taste and the aroma of the food. It was just sumptuous.

I slept well that night but I was feeling a little sick. I had to take one more barb to sort myself out. I only had two days, supply left and I was a bit worried that I might have serious withdrawals and convulse. I was terrified of the fits. I made my mind up to ask David to take me to a doctor. When morning came I just picked at my breakfast.

"Are you feeling OK, John?" David asked.

"David, I'll need to go s-see a doctor to get help when the withdrawals k-kick in."

"That shouldn't be a problem; I'll arrange a visit to our GP this morning, OK?"

"Thanks, David," I said.

"What will you do for the time being?"

"I got some barbs yesterday to get me by for a while. I still have enough to d-do me for a couple of days."

"Will you let me mind them for you, John, so that I can give them to you as needed?"

"No problem," I answered. "I really want to get my life together, David."

"I know that, John; Lorraine and I want to do what we can to help."

Later that morning he took me into town and bought me a whole new set of clothes: a blue bomber jacket, a jumper, two pairs of new jeans, a pair of trainers, a pair of blue shoes, a couple of shirts, a jumper and loads of underwear. I felt so good walking around in my new clothes – a bit of self-respect came back to me that day. I felt like an ordinary citizen – people weren't looking at me thinking, "He is a homeless person" or "He is an addict or alcoholic". I felt good.

The following day George came to stay with us at the house. He was a quiet person who seemed keen to get his life together. I got on well with him from the start.

That afternoon David brought both George and me to the doctor. I went in first and explained to him my history and told him that I was addicted to barbiturates. He listened but was not very sympathetic or understanding. He prescribed medication that I knew would be of little help to me. I reasoned with him but he would not give me anything else. I was disappointed, as I knew that now I would have to "cold turkey" and go through serious withdrawals. George didn't fare any better than I.

I took my last barb before going to bed that evening. Next morning I wasn't feeling well at all. I pushed myself to get up and tried to keep a good attitude. I knew that the withdrawals from barbs could last several weeks.

That evening some girls from the Salvation Army came visiting us to cheer us up. They were kind and very nice. I was feeling terrible. Cold turkey was setting in and my nerves were on edge. My whole inside was shaking, my appetite was gone, and fear and panic that was almost uncontrollable kept seizing me. I tried to stay in the room talking to the visitors but the pressure of conversation and trying to look normal was too much for me. My stutter was completely out of control. My face was beginning to contort, my cheeks were shaking; my lips began to tremble and then – I can remember no more until I came to; feeling like a bomb had gone off in my head. David Lorraine, George, and the visitors were all looking down at me.

"Are you OK, Johnny? We thought that you were dying. Your breathing stopped for a long time and your arms and legs were flapping all over the place." David helped me to my feet and brought me up to my bed. He got me a hot-water bottle and a cup of tea. They gave me one of the tablets the doctor had prescribed for me and then he and Lorraine said a little prayer for me. My whole body was shaking and my mind was full of fear and dread as they prayed for God's peace and protection to be with me. That was nice.

I lay awake for the whole night. The withdrawals got worse and worse. I could see shapes peering out from the corner behind the wardrobe at me; shadows, whispers and shuffling noises came from the other corner. I saw something run across the room at the foot of my bed – it seemed to be laughing at me. I was convinced it was real but I kept telling myself that it was only an effect of the withdrawals. I was so terrified that I had to get out of the house. I got up from my bed, dripping with sweat. Beads of perspiration rolled down my back, neck and legs as I put my clothes on. I got the fright of my life when the door opened. It was George.

"What are you doing, Johnny? I could hear you moving around so I came in to check on you."

"George, I'm g-getting out of here; I can't take the

withdrawals any more. Please tell D-David and Lorraine that I'm sorry."

"No, I can't, John – you see, I want to leave too. I was going to go tomorrow anyway. I didn't tell you, but I had it planned. I'm going to my parents' house down south. I'll just go with you now and head off to my parents later in the day."

I was too sick to argue. I put my few belongings in an old suitcase that David had given me and headed off with George. We managed to slip out of the house without waking anyone. It was about six o'clock in the morning. I knew a doctor that would give me barbs on tick but he wouldn't be there for a few hours yet. I got the Tube to a place where I could get some surgical spirits to tide me over. I got this within an hour of leaving David's house. I went into a public toilet and got some water to mix with it and then drank half of the disgusting mixture. George stayed with me and even walked with me to the doctor's in Willesden. I was there waiting for the doctor when he arrived.

"Come in, Johnny," he said. "You look terrible."

"I am terrible," I replied. "Listen, I have no money and I need some Tuinal. Can you please help me out? I will pay later, I promise."

He argued a bit with me but in the end he gave me a prescription for thirty, three-grain Tuinal. I had obtained a syringe earlier. Once I had the prescription in my hand I felt a little better. I changed it in a chemist's shop down the road and then went to a disused building to have a hit. George came with me; he too had a syringe and a big bottle of water. He wanted a turn-on before he hit the road for his parents' house.

We climbed the four flights of stairs of the disused house and barricaded ourselves into a room, pushing a big wardrobe and some other items against the door to stop anyone coming in and interrupting us. I tried to put the drugs and water into the syringe but I was shaking too much. Even with the surgical spirits inside me I was in a bad way. George mixed it for me as I rolled up my shirtsleeve and worked on getting a vein up. Once I had done that I waited till George was ready. He had put one-and-a-half three-grain Tuinal into the works. I held my arm steady for him as I watched him flick the barrel to get the air bubbles out of it and then squirt a little water out.

"Come on, G-George, hurry up, will you," I said, "I'm sick."

"OK, Johnny; it's ready now . . . calm down, I had to make sure all the air was out of it . . ."

"OK, OK, just get it into me please, will you?" I was getting edgy and impatient. George put the tip of the needle against my scarred vein. He then slid the point of the needle under my skin and pushed it slowly towards the vein. I waited to feel the pop of the needle penetrating it and then said, "It's in, George; draw it back to make sure."

He drew the plunger back and sure enough, there was the dark blood. "Right – put it in, George – slowly does it now, don't let it clog up." George slowly pushed the whole syringe full of barbiturate into my blood stream and instantly all the sickness, fear, panic and dread left me and a wonderful feeling came over me. I was really thankful to be temporarily out of my sickness and withdrawals. I remember thinking to myself, "If only there was a way of getting peace that wouldn't disappear." If there was, I wanted to find it.

George then had a hit of one-and-a-half barbs. I don't remember much after that except that four days later I woke up in the intensive care unit of the Middlesex Hospital in London. I had tubes coming out of every orifice in my body. I can remember seeing a machine at the side of the bed that was attached in some way to my mouth. It was pumping up and down and pushing air into my lungs, then taking it out again. I remember looking at it and thinking, "That's strange – what is it there for?" I must have drifted off again for a while. I finally came to and the doctors explained to me the miracle of my still being alive.

It turned out that someone had seen George and I go into the disused building that we were injecting the drugs in. They called the police. When the police arrived they could not get past the barricade, so they called the fire brigade. When the fire brigade came they raised the big ladder up to the window of the room we were in; then, having broken the window, they climbed in. They found both George and I overdosed and apparently lifeless, lying unconscious on the floor. The firemen picked us up, and on their shoulders they carried us down to the waiting ambulance.

The doctor told me that I had been in a coma for over three days. "You were at the point of death a number of times, young man," he said. "If the police had not been called you would be dead, there is no doubt about it. Your pal is still unconscious; he is further down the ward. He will be all right, though. You both took enough barbiturates to kill a horse. You are one lucky man to be alive."

I rested all that day and night. The next morning I asked for my clothes because I wanted to leave. The staff at the hospital argued with me and told me I would be foolish to leave as I was still very sick and in need of treatment.

"Your whole system was shutting down, John," they said. "You need time to recover."

"No," I said, "I want to leave."

"If you leave you will have to sign a form stating that you left against medical advice."

"OK, I'll sign it but I want out. Please g-get me my clothes." They told me that they searched high and low for my clothes but could not find them.

"I need some clothes to go out in," I insisted. "You're just p-playing for time trying to keep me here against my will." I then ripped all the tubes out from my body and caused a great commotion.

"OK, OK, John – you can go. We'll find some clothes for you." The hospital staff managed to find an old coat that was about five sizes too big for me. Long, baggy trousers and a shirt big enough for a man twice my size.

One of the nurses pulled the curtain around my bed and waited outside for me while I got dressed. When I was ready to go they brought the form for me to sign. The nurse took me to see George before I left. He was still looking very poorly but I knew he would be fine. I wished him well and left the hospital. I felt no regret at leaving George there; he was just another one of the acquaintances that I met on my journey of life; there were no bonds or promises to keep. We had kept each other company for just part of that journey.

HELPING HANDS

It was cold and dark outside, I looked terrible, and now I was dressed like a tramp as well. I lived like a rat on the streets for the next three weeks, begging for a living, staying in the shadows of London's West End and sleeping on cardboard in doorways and down dangerous alleys; I had thrown caution to the wind. Many times I was threatened; sometimes I was beaten up. I managed to cut down on using barbs and took a lot of methadone amps and heroin. Heroin always made me sick and was never my first choice of drug, but I would use it when I could get nothing else.

One night I lay down to sleep in an old shed. It was freezing and snow was blowing in through the doorway. I thought of David and Lorraine's nice home down by Portobello Market. I wondered if they would take me in if I went back to them. I was desperate; at that moment I could not take any more of living on the streets. I made my mind up I would go and ask them to take me back on the following morning.

I didn't sleep at all that night, so as soon as the tubes were running I travelled on the Circle Line for a few hours. Then at about nine in the morning I made my way to their house. I was nervous; maybe they would reject me – maybe I had hurt them too much by leaving the way I had. I was very self-conscious in the old clothes I was wearing. I stood outside the door of their house for quite a while trying to work up the nerve to knock. Finally I reached out and knocked hard on the door. I took a deep breath and stood back. "What will be, will be," I said to myself as I stood waiting. After what seemed like an age the door opened and both David and Lorraine stood there. For a split second they stared at me. Then they rushed out, swept me up in their arms and pulled me close to them.

"Oh John, it's so good to see you! We were so worried about you. We have been praying for you." I was very relieved by their response and it was wonderful to see these two lovely Christian people again. If ever I experienced unconditional love in my life it was at that moment.

WALKING FREE

Rehabilitation Centre

David and Lorraine took me into their home and gave me another chance. They gave me a good telling off for my behaviour and made me promise that I wouldn't leave in that way again. These people really cared for me. I wasn't used to that kind of love, not on the streets of London.

They brought me to a different doctor and this one gave me medication that helped me through my withdrawals. David then arranged for me to go to a rehabilitation centre near Uxbridge. It was a lovely big house with a huge garden. There was a river that we could fish and canoe in. I was interviewed and accepted.

I went back with David and Lorraine for a few more days and then moved down to the centre outside Uxbridge.

I settled down quite well, even though there were many things I did not agree with on the programme. If any of the lads on the programme was not sure of their sexuality they were allowed to experiment by cross-dressing or putting make-up on. Sometimes these big lads built like rugby players could be seen going around with mascara, lipstick and rouge on their faces, and wearing nice necklaces. To me it was ridiculous. One or two gay men came to the centre and they loved the chance to put on make-up and they encouraged others to try it also. It got really confusing when the trustees of the centre decided to take women in as well as men. We then had guys dressed as women, women dressed as men, sneaking off together to have sex in the shed at the end of the garden.

Jealousies amongst the men and women came to a head at the Tuesday and Thursday confrontation groups. During those group sessions you were allowed to deal with any upset or anger you may have, although negative feelings were not tolerated at other times. The meetings were explosive and very upsetting for many of the people staying there. The hatred and venom that was expressed was sometimes quite frightening. I witnessed many men and women break down after having a barrage of often misplaced or misdirected feelings fired at them from other members of the community.

Mick was a great big Scottish guy who had a family waiting for him when he finished the programme. He talked all the time about his family, how he wanted to be a good dad to his children and husband to his wife one day. He got so upset and confused with some of the goings-on that he left the house. He returned, however, after a few days, pleading to be accepted back in. We were told to make the decision as to whether he should be taken back or not. The staff said it was our house and therefore our responsibility.

A meeting was called and a vote was taken. Each of us was given a piece of paper on which we were to write, "Yes, Mick can come back", or "No, Mick cannot come back". I voted "Yes". I didn't expect anyone to vote otherwise. Mick was a man who wanted to rebuild his life and go back to his family. He had realised his mistake in leaving and was brave enough to return. The staff collected the votes. They went out of the room, counted them and within minutes they were back. Pete, a senior staff member, announced the result of the vote.

"The house has voted not to take Mick back into the house. We will inform him."

Pete and the other staff members went to the office where Mick was waiting and told him the bad news. We could hear him pleading with the staff to let him stay. He was in tears and completely dejected when he left the house. There was no laughter there that night. The responsibility for Mick's future had been in our hands and we had made a judgement. Selfishly I was relieved that I had voted for him to be re-admitted.

Mick was found dead a couple of days later. He had overdosed and his body was found in a little bed-sit in London. I represented the house at his funeral, as nobody else wanted to go. The day was damp and cold; there was only a small handful of people at the graveside. It was one of the saddest funerals I have ever attended. Mick's wife fell on her knees at the graveside. She was wailing, "Oh Mick, Mick, come back to us, come back to us!" Her two children were crying and trying to pull her back from the grave. They were only four and six years of age. We adults eventually had to hold her or she would have fallen into the grave after the coffin.

When I returned to the house, some of the others could not look me in the eye. I guessed that they had voted "No" to Mick returning to the house. Dianne the director called a special group meeting to try to sort out the mess. We were meant to be rehabilitating but I, for one, was getting more screwed-up.

"We're going to have a sensitivity group," Dianne announced. These were sometimes marathon sessions, lasting more than twenty-four hours. We would bring our duvets into the lounge, to sleep in. During these sensitivity groups we would play nice music, tell each other in turn nice things about each other. We would do relaxation exercises, massage each other, and practise levitation. The latter was achieved by each of us taking turns to lie down on our backs while six or seven of the others stood around and put one finger each under the person lying down. He or she was then lifted up towards the ceiling while some nice new-age music played in the background. I didn't like it; it was really spooky. Dianne the director would then start sensing messages coming to her from dead people. She would say that she could sense certain dead people in the room. During this group she started saying that she could sense Mick in the room. "He has his hand on my shoulder," she said. I looked around the room; everyone's eyes were transfixed, looking at Dianne's shoulder. They all believed her.

"I'm sorry, Mick," one of the girls shouted out. "I'm sorry for not voting for you to stay." Everyone was crying now. Dianne then piped up and said, "I sense Mick is saying it's OK, that he's in a better place now and we're not to feel guilty."

What a load of manipulative rubbish, I thought to myself. I wanted to leave the house but I had nowhere to go.

Yet the atmosphere did improve after the sensitivity group and I stayed for nearly a year. I was allowed to go out for a drink at weekends, as a privilege. I was told that I could control my drinking. But this was more rubbish – from day one, I drank more than my allowance of beer. Indeed I began to buy vodka and drink it outside the house. I managed to hide that well for a while.

I was eventually given the responsibility of covering for some weekends as a voluntary staff member. On the Friday of one of these weekends a 25-year-old lad called Steven walked out. Steven was a great fellow, always on for a laugh, but he, like some of the rest of us, was struggling with the régime of the house. The next morning I received a phone call from the local police telling me that Steven had been caught breaking into the local doctor's surgery. He was now in the police cells. I told the police that I would inform the senior staff member who was on call for the weekend. I phoned the covering senior staff member and told him what had happened. That was my responsibility taken care of.

Monday morning came and Dianne called me into her office. "Sit down, John," she said. "Tell me exactly what happened before Steven left on Friday night. Then tell me exactly how you dealt with the situation. I want to know why you did not inform me about him being locked up in the cells in Uxbridge police station. By the way, John – before you tell me these things, you need to know that Steven is dead. He hanged himself with his shoelaces in the cell."

I was completely shocked at this news. I stuttered and stumbled my way through my explanation of the happenings on the weekend. Dianne went as far as to say that she believed I was responsible for Steven's death. I could not handle that guilt trip. I did not have the strength of character at the time to confront her about this allegation. Instead I took it in and buried the anger and misplaced guilt.

That weekend I left the house. I swore to myself that I would never go to rehab again.

Chapter Fifteen
We Are the Champions

Back in Hospital

It wasn't long before I ended up on the streets. I told myself that I did not want to live in a world where people treated me like that. I carried a lot of guilt around about Steven's death until eventually I gave in and started taking drugs again. In no time at all, I was worse than I had ever been. During this time I was put on a methadone maintenance course by a drug clinic in London. I was also addicted to Valium and alcohol again. I got so bad that a doctor reserved me a bed in St Bernard's psychiatric hospital just off the Uxbridge Road in London.

I tried my best to improve while I was in there. In all, I spent about six weeks on the ward. I came off all drugs and began to work-out by running around the field at the front of the ward. I have always been a good runner – out running I can be alone with my thoughts. Even then I could run for miles once I got into my rhythm.

I wasn't aware of it, but at that time psychiatric hospitals used to hold Sports Days. Each year a few of the patients were chosen to represent their hospital by taking part in the annual Sports Day. There was a Cup at stake and this Cup was much coveted by the different hospitals.

Tim was a psychiatric nurse on our ward. He was Irish and loved sports. I began to notice him watching me train in the field outside the hospital ward. I was fast and I had the endurance for longer distances. One day he came out and called me to him.

"John," he said, "I've been watching you train over the last few weeks. It is amazing how far you have progressed in that time. You are a great runner. How do you fancy taking part in the inter-hospital Sports Day representing St Bernard's hospital?"

"I would love to," I replied.

"Great," Tim answered. "I'll introduce you to the rest of the team tomorrow."

The next morning the rest of the team, who had been selected from the other wards, came to meet me. They were a lovely bunch of girls and lads but some of them were really not very well. They reminded me of the Dozy Dozen from St Brendan's Hospital in Dublin. Most of them were on heavy doses of Largactyl, Meloril or similar drugs. They were like robots walking around. One of them was very fast, however. He was a black West Indian lad called Alan. Tim brought Alan down to the track with me and pointed him in the direction he wanted him to run.

"John, you run with him and we'll see who can go the fastest. The winner will go in for the one hundred metres on Sports Day."

Alan and I stood at the start line. "Are you ready, lads?" said Tim. "You have to run as far as that tree down there, OK? That's about one hundred metres. Do you both understand?"

"Yes, Tim," I answered.

"Alan, do you understand?"

"Yes, Tim," he replied.

"Right, on your marks; get set – GO." Alan and I took off across the field. He was built like a tank but he ran like a hare. He was like lightning. I managed to keep up with him until the end, but he pipped me at the post. We rested for a half-hour and then did the same with the two hundred metres. I won that. By the end of the day we both knew which races we were running.

Champions

The Psychiatric Hospitals Sports Day finally arrived. We were all excited. Tim, Alan and I, with the rest of the team, climbed aboard the St Bernard's bus and headed off to the sports ground where the events were to take place. The hospital gave us kits to run in. God had blessed us with a hot summer's day and everything was perfect. Tim pulled me to one side and said that he had put me in for a couple of extra races as he didn't feel we had a chance to win the Cup if some of the others ran.

"If we have two of you in each race we have a great chance," he said. "St Bernard's have never been in with a better chance of winning. Are you up for it, John?"

"Tim, is it fair?" I asked. "I mean, I'm in St B-Bernard's for addiction but I'm not addicted right now. Everyone else here has some s-serious psychiatric illness. Is it fair if I run in so many races without a similar handicap?"

"You're a patient at St Bernard's, aren't you?" he said.

"Yes I am," I answered.

"Well, then, you qualify. End of story, OK? Now get on with winning some races for us."

I must admit I felt a little bit guilty but I decided to give each race my best. Our team sat and watched the opening ceremony in the hot sunshine. Because of all the excitement we forgot to tell those on Largactyl to stay out of the sun. The sun reacts with Largactyl and burns anyone who is on it. Alan and many of the others on our team got quite burnt. Belatedly, we put lots of sun protection cream on everyone and tried to keep everyone under cover when they weren't taking part in a race. One of them had to pull out of the sack race, so I was entered in his place.

The 100 metre race was the first event that day. Tim led Alan to the start line, pointed him in the right direction and waited for the gun to go off. Alan knew exactly what to do. The man held up the starter pistol.

"On your marks, get set . . ." BANG! The gun went off and Alan was gone like a bat out of hell. He left everyone else behind by about ten yards and easily won the race.

Next was the 200 metre race. I got in position; Tim was standing beside me. He was more excited than anybody was. I had noticed the rivalry between the staff from the other hospitals and him. I could see that for them there was more than a cup at stake here.

"Right John," he said, "go for it, right? You should win this easily, but don't use all your energy because you have the

1,000 metres to do next, and then the sack race straight after that. Then if you're not too tired you are in for the egg-and-spoon race as well."

"Tim, l-leave me alone – you're exhausting me. You're p-putting me under p-pressure by just telling me."

"Sorry, John – but you've got to pace yourself so that you can run all the races and do well."

"OK, Tim – don't worry, I'll be fine. I'll j-just do the best I can," I answered. "Up the Irish, Tim!"

"Ah pog mo thone!" he said, which means, "Kiss my bum" in Gaelic. I ran the 200 metre race and won without straining myself too much. Everyone was thrilled. We were beginning to believe that we could win the Cup this year. I had a half-hour break before my next race. I rested in the shade, stretched my legs and drank plenty of cold water.

Ten minutes before the 1,000 metre race I began to jog slowly round the field to warm up. Then I lined up for the race. I focused myself. My plan was to take it easy for the first 400 metres. If anyone went out fast I should be able to tell if they had endurance or if they would faze out in the second half of the race. The gun went off and away we went. Several of the runners ran ahead of me but I just let them go. I didn't let them get too far ahead but I didn't tire myself trying to keep up. At around the 300 mark, I passed one of them by. At the 500 metre stage, two of them were still ahead of me by about ten metres. I kept my pace and by 800 metres, only one of them was still ahead. I could tell that he was tiring, though; he was losing his rhythm. I slowly reeled him in and sprinted the last 50 metres to win the race easily.

Tim and our team were ecstatic. "Yahoo!" "What a race!" "Well done, John . . ." Everyone came around me hugging me and patting me on the back. There was real camaraderie amongst us. I noticed Tim looking at his rivals with a smirk on his face. "Oh you're a marvel, John," he said to me. "That was a brilliant run. If we keep this up the Cup will be ours."

They were just about to start the sack race as the 1000 metre race was finishing. I had to go straight over and get into a sack and hop 100 metres. Alan, and Mary, one of the girls from the team, were in this race also. Alan was like a kangaroo, he and Mary did very well. Alan came second and Mary came third; I kept falling over and came fifth. Still, we picked up a lot of points towards the Cup.

The egg-and-spoon race came later. I had time to recover from the races I had run so far. I was also able to practise and by the time the race began I was confident I could do well.

"John, if we come in the first three in this race we cannot be beaten," Tim said. "The cup will be ours."

"Right, I'll do my best." Both Alan and I were in the race. The team lined the 100 metres to cheer us on. We held our spoons, placed our potatoes (which we used instead of eggs) on the spoons and waited for the start.

"Ready? Get set . . . " BANG! We all took off as fast as we could. Both Alan and I got a good start. We dropped our potatoes a few times, having to stop and pick them up before proceeding. The team cheered as we raced towards the finishing line. Alan crossed first and I came in second. The Cup was ours; St Bernard's was the champion psychiatric hospital in London at sports that year. Oh the jubilation! Tim was almost out of control. "Ye boyo, John! We did it! The Cup is ours." He kept hugging us all. There were one or two races after that but the Cup was ours.

Four o'clock came and it was time for the Cup to be presented to us. Our team was called forward and some official guy presented us with the Cup. I looked at the team. There was such life in their faces; great big smiles on every one of them. The man who presented the Cup to us spoke through a microphone. "The champions and winners of the Cup in the Inter-Hospital Sports Event 1981 are the patients of St Bernard's Hospital." The cup was presented to Tim. He kissed it and then held it up for everyone to see. Oh we cheered so loud and so long – we didn't want the moment to go away. Some of the team were crying with joy. We were each presented with a medal before we took the Cup on a victory circuit of the sports field. What a day it was.

"It's good to b-be alive, Alan," I said as I passed the cup to him. He was smiling and laughing and holding the cup up high.

WALKING FREE

Today we were champions. Psychiatric patients, addicts, staff members, black, white – a motley crew, but still champions, joined together in a common purpose: to do the best we could, regardless of background or ethnic origin. No one could take that away from us. We drove back to the ward singing songs and congratulating each other. There was great excitement as we presented the Cup at the ward. Everyone came to congratulate us, all the staff, recovering alcoholics, addicts and others took it in turns to clap us on the back and join in the celebration. We weren't patients today – we were champions; we had achieved and excelled. This was life.

Asian Children at Risk

I finished my stay in St Bernard's shortly after the Sports Day. Several of us had grown quite close while we were there. Barry was one of the patients. He suffered from anorexia but he was a great chef. On the evening I was leaving he prepared a lovely meal for about ten of us who had got quite close. We wished each other well that night and all my hospital friends encouraged me to "go for it". "You have such potential, John," they said. Well, I really wanted to go for it. I wasn't convinced that I knew how, though. Tim had helped me achieve in hospital but I had no Tim outside.

I left the hospital and went to live in Southall. I got a job as a community worker with Asian Children at Risk. I think they were at risk when they were with me. I had some unconventional ways of dealing with problems – like the time we had a wasps' nest in the back garden. Everyone tried to get rid of the wasps, poking sticks down the nest, only to be met with and stung by angry wasps. They tried to set it on fire and that didn't work. I came along and told them that I would deal with the dreaded wasps once and for all. All my Asian colleagues gathered around as I made a pipe-bomb. It was over a foot long and was made of thick metal. I was able to get the ingredients from a local hardware shop. I put a long trail of the explosive on the outside of the wasps' nest. Then I stuck the bomb into the top of the nest as far as it would go. Having made sure that everyone was at a safe distance, I lit the trail and stood back. The trail burned away quite quickly; then there was this terrific explosion: BOOM. We waited a moment and then went out to examine the scene. There was a big hole in the ground where the wasps' nest used to be but there was not a wasp to be seen anywhere. That was the end of the nest.

During 1982 Britain saw many race riots and Southall was no exception. A young man called Blair Peach had died as a result of a beating at the hands of the police; anger flared and eventually spilled over into riots. I foolishly used my experience to teach many how to make petrol bombs. We made dozens of them, hiding them in milk crates down back alleys, pulling them out as we battled and fought with the hundreds of police sent to break up the riots. It was crazy: a skinny little Irish guy leading a gang of Punjabi and Urdu-speaking Asians in an attack on British police. I felt like a mixture of Michael Collins (one of the fathers of the Republic of Ireland), Michael Caine as he appeared in "Zulu" and a vigilante Ghandi all rolled into one.

I thank God that no one that I worked with was hurt. Yes, Asian Children at Risk would be far safer without me. I was also drinking heavily at this time. Eventually I fell back on drugs but not on the needle again. Nevertheless, from that time on in my life, I made real efforts to get better.

Chapter Sixteen
Death of My Dad

Daddy's Dead

I was fired from my job in Southall. I was sorry, as I had made some good friends amongst the Asian people. I made my way back up to Harlesden in northwest London and stayed in an old Irish doss house. The place was disgusting. the owner was a man from the west of Ireland named Mr Harrison. He drove a brown Rolls Royce. Every day he parked it outside the bay window of the room that I shared with two other hard-drinking and hard-working Irish road workers. I was annoyed with this man as I felt that he was taking advantage of poor Irishmen who were down on their luck. I would look at that Rolls Royce and say to myself that one day I would be able to get myself a nice car, and live in a nice house. One day I would be free of drugs and drink and I'd help others who were down on their luck.

The place was filthy. The scum of the earth lived and worked here: old perverts, dying homosexuals, lonely alcoholics. Sad people, all of them. Each one had a story to tell. The toilets were usually broken, so everyone used the sinks in their rooms, which resulted in each room smelling strongly of urine. There was no heat, so we froze in the winter. Any money we had we drank. We worked whenever we could with subcontractors or Irish travellers, putting down crazy paving or tarmacadam. We usually earned about fifteen pounds a day. Sometimes the travellers wouldn't pay you and there was not much you could do about it.

I had begun to attend Alcoholics Anonymous. I was trying to get things together; I was making efforts; I could not take much more of this life. I took a job in a precision tool-making company as a labourer. The money was less than I got on the dole but at least I was out earning and keeping busy. My self-esteem began to grow. I was getting a week here, two weeks there without drink. I was still addicted to Valium and I would spend most evenings out seeing doctors for it. I must have attended about ten doctors at the same time to keep me supplied. I was making an effort, though, and I was making slow progress. I began to train and run a bit, even through the on-going Valium abuse.

On the 31st October 1983, Halloween night, I was sitting upstairs in the room that my friends Mayo Mick and English Dave occupied when someone came to the door and told me that there was a phone call for me. The phone was down on the first floor of the big old doss-house. "Who could that be?" I wondered. "Nobody ever phones me. My family don't even know that I live here." I made my way down to the phone and picking up the receiver, said in a cautious tone, "Hello, this is John. Who is speaking?"

"Hello John, I've been trying to get your address and phone number all day." I froze, recognising the voice of one of my sisters. I knew something must be wrong for them to trace me to this doss-house.

"W-what is it Geraldine?" I asked.

"John, I am afraid I have some bad news for you. Daddy is dead, he died earlier today." I was stunned.

"Daddy's dead? No, he can't be," I thought; "he can't die until I am well and he is proud of me and we're all friends again."

"John, are you still there?" my sister said.

"Yes, I am here."

"John, the family have talked things over and we all feel that it might be best if you didn't come home for the funeral. We are afraid that you might get stoned or drunk and upset mammy or something. John, we all love you and want to see you, but . . ."

DEATH OF MY DAD

"It's OK, I understand," I answered. I always understand, I thought to myself; that's part of my problem. When will someone else understand that I want to be at my dad's funeral? He is my father, my dad; I love him too. I never said a word or made a scene, though. I just said to my sister that I would like to be able to go. I felt like I needed permission to go to my own dad's funeral, like I didn't have a right to go. I felt weak, a complete failure, beaten, defeated; life had beaten me to the point that I could not stand up for myself even if I tried. I didn't know how to stand up for myself. I never knew how to stand up for myself. I was so used to upsetting people and being in the wrong that I didn't know how to communicate with others how I really felt.

My sister's voice interrupted my troubled thoughts and emotions. "If you do come, John – and we would prefer that you didn't – you would need to go back to England straight after the funeral."

"Right," I said. "Bye for now." I put the phone down, went into my own room and cracked up. I completely lost it. I broke down and wept; I smashed chairs and a table against the wall.

After a while I calmed down. My dream of seeing my dad and making him proud of me could never be realised now. I had failed him and I could not even go to his funeral. I felt so ashamed, so guilty for letting him down.

I tried to understand how my family felt. I knew that it was hard for them to have a brother who was addicted; I had caused a lot of grief over the years. But I was hurt by what they had said and began to feel bitter. I was also bitter and unforgiving towards myself. I wanted to go to my father's funeral and I planned to try and get the money from somewhere so that I could go. I decided that I would not tell my family that I was going; I would simply turn up at the church and leave afterwards.

I went to different people asking for money to help me get home to Ireland. Surely someone would give me money to go to my dad's funeral . . . I went to an Irish Catholic charity in Hammersmith, where I knew they sometimes gave money to people in trouble. When I told them what I needed money for, they didn't believe me but thought I was trying to con them. I was shocked that they thought I would lie about my dad's death just to get money out of them. I then asked the owner of the Irish doss-house I was staying in. He and his wife refused to help me and told me I was a dosser and a tramp; that I was a shame to my family and in no way would they help me. I tried everything to get money to go home. All it would take was about £20 but I could not get it. I finally resigned myself to the reality that I would not be able to go.

The morning of my dad's funeral I begged and borrowed enough money for two bottles of cheap wine. I went down a back alley and began to drown my sorrows. Shortly afterwards an old tramp that I knew called Wally came along and sat down beside me on the dried mud. I shared the cheap wine with him and chatted. Eventually I looked at my watch; it was just after ten o'clock in the morning. My sister had told me that some of my brother's friends were going to carry the coffin out of the house and down the road to the chapel. I pictured them standing with my father's coffin on their shoulders and carrying it out of our house in Dublin. The tears began to flow down my cheeks. I missed my da and I knew I'd never see him again. I should be there; I should be carrying his coffin . . . I began to sob. Wally looked at me with compassion in his eyes and asked me what was wrong.

"My da died and he's getting b-buried right now in Dublin and I should be there," I said.

Street people and tramps are hurt people and they don't usually show compassion to each other, but Wally was different; he had been living rough in doss-houses, spikes and on the streets for a long time. He was in his 60s. Wally wasn't crazy: he was an old man of the road; he had chosen his lifestyle and he had street wisdom like no one else I had met. I didn't want to be with anybody that morning but when Wally turned up I was grateful. He put his arm around me and held me as I cried. He comforted me and helped me grieve.

"John," Wally said, "your father would be happy to see you get your life together and come off the streets. You should go home to Ireland, son, and get off the drugs and drink. If you don't you'll die John. Your da wouldn't want that, would he?"

DEATH OF MY DAD

"No, he wouldn't," I replied.

Wally rolled an old Holborn cigarette. "Here John, smoke that. And take a drink of the wine, it will help you." I remember thinking that it was funny how Wally advised me to stop drinking and then in the next breath offered me a slug out of the bottle. He didn't have to explain to me that it was OK *for now* to drink.

I relaxed a bit more after that and began to tell Wally about my da, how he was a self-made man who had known great success in business but that the drink had taken it all from him. "My da lost his high-flying job, Wally," I said, "but he wouldn't give in – he kept t-trying to stop drinking and he worked at whatever he could to p-pay the bills. He took on a job as a petrol-pump attendant and then in a b-book publishing company. Before he died he had cut down a lot on his drinking and d-drove a hackney cab around Dublin. He prayed a lot too before he died – he also went to the church most evenings – I'm sure he was p-praying for me . . ." Memories flashed across my mind of my da. In some of the memories he was smiling and laughing, while in others he was lonely, sad, even tormented. "My da's life was a sad one, Wally. He d-did the best he c-could for us all; he provided well for us as a f-family, but I believe that inside he was a hurting, lonely and bankrupt man. Life didn't work very well for him in the end, Wally – hopefully he is in a better place now."

"I'm sure he is, John," Wally said as he patted me on my back to comfort me.

My da's death and the fact that I missed his funeral left a scar in my very soul. I was in turmoil on the inside but tried to remain calm and confident on the surface. I needed drugs and drink to maintain my outer composure and calm the storms on the inside. I was living a lie to others and cheating myself out of being true to myself. I carried so much baggage of hurt, pain and rejection that I didn't know who I was any more. I often found myself saying things to others that I didn't believe, just to please them and keep the peace. I couldn't take any more.

WALKING FREE

I lived in this state for a year before the compass of my heart began to point towards home. I needed my mother and I needed my family. I had nowhere else left to go. I had tried everything to live a so-called normal life but I needed a rest and I needed love and acceptance. Thoughts of suicide were beginning to flash across my mind quite a lot in those days; I pushed them away as quickly as I could and focused on getting home.

Coming Home

I decided to come home without telling anybody. Not that I was planning a surprise; I was simply afraid that if I told them I was coming they would try to stop me. I worked with sub-contractors on building sites for a little while, even though I was quite sick, and managed to keep enough money for my one-way ticket back to Dublin. I went around my various suppliers and got enough drugs to keep me going for a week or so when I got back to Ireland. At last I packed my meagre belongings and headed into Euston station to go home.

While I stood on the platform waiting for the train I recalled the day I came to London hoping to get my life together. I was now going back home in a worse mess than when I had arrived and with less hope for my future. Yet I still had my resolve to keep going, even though it was getting weaker now. This weakening frightened me. I was afraid to think about it or about failing any more. I would keep going. I'd give it one more try.

We travelled by train overnight to Holyhead, where we boarded the boat for Dublin. I found a quiet corner and had a sleep for an hour. When I woke up I bought a half bottle of cheap vodka at the duty-free shop on the boat. I went out on deck, put my woolly hat on and pulled my jacket collar up around my neck to keep the cold north wind out. I found a place to sit at the front of the boat and, sitting down, I took out my vodka from under my jacket. I promised myself that I would not get drunk. I sipped the vodka as I watched the lights of Dublin city come into focus. I wondered what my family's reaction would be when I arrived home: not too pleased, I expected. I thought about the "mailer" tree where my friends and I used watch this very boat going back and forth from

DEATH OF MY DAD

Britain and how much we envied the people travelling on it then. Now I was one of those travellers and I wished I could return to the happier days of my childhood. "Life sure is queer," I said aloud as I stood up and went back to the warmth of the bar. I found an almost full pint glass of Guinness that someone had left behind, so I sat down, rolled a cigarette and went to the window to drink it while I waited for the boat to dock. "Please God, let my family accept me when I go home and make me happy." The boat was now docked so I finished the pint of Guinness in one swallow, stuck the fag in my mouth and walked down the gangplank into Dublin. There were many people waiting to greet relatives and friends as they disembarked. I put my hand into my pocket and took out a few Valium and swallowed them. They would begin to affect me by about the time I arrived home at my ma's. "They will give me confidence," I reassured myself.

I got on the 44a bus for my mother's house at about 7 a.m. It was raining and cold. At that time it was still permissible to smoke upstairs on the bus, so up I went. I pulled my woolly hat down around my ears and hid as much of my face as possible with my collar. I didn't want to meet anybody that I knew. The bus passed my old school; we were nearly there and I was very nervous. I pressed my upper arm against my chest so that I could feel and be comforted by the still half-full bottle of vodka in my inside pocket. The bus pulled in at the last stop. I got off, threw my little bag with all my earthly belongings in it over my shoulder and headed towards my mother's house. I walked down the back alley behind our house, stopping briefly outside Mrs Ailward's garage to take one last swig of vodka before arriving home. I climbed over our back wall and walked down the garden and through the side passage to the front door. I put some chewing gum in my mouth to disguise the smell of booze, combed my hair, straightened my wrinkled jacket and then knocked softly on the front door. I was terrified and half-hoped no one would hear my knock. There was no answer. I stepped back and looked up at my mother's bedroom window. The curtains were drawn. She must be asleep still, I decided. I didn't want to wake her, so I went around to the back of the house and climbed up on our kitchen roof and came in through the open window of the back bedroom.

I crept slowly and quietly through the bedroom and out into the upstairs passage that led to my mother's room. I gently squeezed her door open and craned my head round to peep in. There she was, sound asleep. I could smell the old familiar fragrance of my mother – a nice mixture of 4711 perfume, Knights Castile soap and other womanly things. She didn't hear me come in to her room so I slowly and carefully sat down on my father's side of the bed. I reached out my hand and felt the pillow where he used to lay his head. I thought I detected his smell too: Brilliantine hair oil, pipe tobacco and King Edward cigars. I was choking back the tears when my mother stirred, opened her eyes and looked up at me. I quickly pulled my hand back from my father's pillow and looked at her. A big smile spread across her face and she said, "Eddie." In a moment, as she became fully conscious, she realised her mistake; that it wasn't her husband but her son, John, who sat before me. My heart had risen when she smiled, only to sink again as I watched her expression change.

"Oh John," she said, "I thought you were your father – oh, you're the image of him." She wasn't happy to see me, I could tell that. She sat up in her bed and looking at me she said, "Where have you come from, John? – You look terrible."

"Ma," I blurted out, "I want to come home. I can't live in London any more – I'm so unhappy over there. I have nowhere else to go, ma. Can I come home?"

She looked at me without saying a word for what seemed like a long time. Then she said, "Come here to me, son," and opening up her arms she gave me one of those great big mother hugs. I was overwhelmed. I just snuggled into her and cried my eyes out. "Do you know, son, it took me hours to give birth to you, over half-an-hour just to deliver your head, you were such a big baby, and you've been causing me pain ever since. I love you, though, and you can stay here with me." She paused for a moment and then she said, "But you'll have to get help for your addiction – you can't live here and keep drinking and drugging, OK?"

DEATH OF MY DAD

"OK, ma," I said, "I'll try my best."

"You will have to pay your way as well, John – you da's not here any more and I can't afford to keep you."

"I'll find work, ma," I promised.

"You can have your old box-room back, John. Go and put your things in there and have a bath – you look like you need one. I'll make us some porridge for breakfast."

I had a lovely long soak in *our* bath in *our* bathroom. I was home. I enjoyed spending the day with my mother; we talked a lot and I promised much. I was determined to try my best to get my life in order.

The next day I went about getting myself sorted out. My first calls were to doctors; I visited three of them and secured prescriptions for Valium, enough to get me by. Then I signed on the dole. There was not much work going in Dublin at that time so I had to find work for myself.

I searched around our house for a fork and a bucket. When the tide was out I went to dig rag- and lug-worms along the shore. Fishermen used these and usually bought them from shops in Dublin city. I made sure I got really big worms. I wrapped a dozen of them in seaweed and rolled them up in newspaper. I made lots of these packs and went around the fishing tackle shops in Dublin and sold them. They were so pleased with my worms that I got contracts to dig hundreds of worms for them. I earned enough from this to support myself and fund my drinking; there was even enough left over to pay my ma money every week for my keep.

I put a bit of money to one side and when I had enough I bought a set of ladders. I had no way of getting them home so I carried them on my shoulders the six miles to our house. I then visited all the houses in our area and got myself a window cleaning round. I did very well at this, sometimes earning as much as ten pounds an hour. Then I got into gardening, painting and decorating. I even at one stage got a Toyota Crown automatic car and had two lads working for me. I would go out in the morning to clean the windows. I was often very sick from drinking and drugging, so I would literally shake and rattle up the ladder. When I got paid for the first job I would run down to the off-licence and buy a small bottle of vodka. I then walked across the road from the off-licence and drank the bottle of vodka in one go before returning to continue cleaning windows. As soon as I got more money I would return to the off-licence and buy more vodka.

I tried to stop drinking by taking more Valium; this involved attending about seven doctors in Dublin every week. Three of them were in one surgery and each was unaware that the other doctors in the practice were prescribing for me also. At the same time several local chemists gave me some over the counter, without any prescription. One chemist gave me one hundred, 5mg Valium for four pounds and another gave me fifty, for two pounds. I visited these about two or three times a week. In total I was taking one hundred Valium a day, sometimes one-hundred-and-fifty. Doctor O'Driscoll, our family doctor, had a serious talk with me during this time. I would go and see him if I was genuinely sick. He wouldn't give me any drugs; he was a good man and gave me some wise advice. "John," he said, "if you keep going on the way you have been you will be dead within a year. You need to stop drinking and taking drugs."

"I'll try, doctor," I told him. I was getting a lot of pains in my liver and kidneys and had begun to feel very concerned about my health. The Valium was having a strange effect on me. The more I took, the more nervous and sick I felt. If I tried to stop I experienced serious withdrawals and took fits. I was very frightened; I felt that I couldn't keep taking them and yet I couldn't stop.

My mother was upset with me again. "John," she begged, "please stop taking drugs and drinking. It killed your father and your friends and it will kill you if you don't stop." My brothers and sisters were also fed up with me. I was a pest and a burden to them all, or so I felt.

"I p-promise you, ma, I will stop," I declared. "I'll go into the drug clinic and ask them to help me." At this stage I was sick, very sick.

The next day I visited the drug clinic in Pearse Street, Dublin, where a Doctor O'Connor arranged for me to go into

DEATH OF MY DAD

St Michael's ward at Beaumont Hospital. Within a week I was in the ward. I was treated very well there; the nurses and wardens were amazing. I was ready to go home after six weeks, drug- and drink-free again.

The day before I was due to leave I stood at the window of the first-floor ward and looked out towards a big old scarred and weather-beaten tree. As I thought of my release on the following day I felt terrified. I didn't know if I could make it. I was thirty-two years of age and afraid of life. I didn't sleep very well that night. I made a plan to get a taxi home – I knew that I wouldn't make it on the bus; I would stop for drink or drugs or maybe both. I didn't want to – I really didn't want to – but I was not in control. I realised that I didn't know how to live without drugs and drink. All the poor guys and girls in here with me were in the same boat; there was no hope for us. Many of them had AIDS. We were like the walking dead. Rehab didn't work, psychiatrists couldn't help, drugs didn't get me stoned any more and drink made me sick. I felt as if nobody wanted me. I just didn't have the ability to stop and get off this horrible merry-go-round. I had too much pain and too much hurt.

As it drew near time to leave the next day, two of the nurses, Eileen and Margaret, called me over to the office to talk to me.

"John, we don't want to see you back in here again," Margaret said. "You're a lovely person, John, and we know that you can make it. You out of all the people who have come in here can make it. We both believe that, don't we, Eileen?"

"We do, John," Eileen said.

"John's taxi is outside," Henry the warden called out. He was a great guy and I knew I would miss him.

"Goodbye, John – remember, we don't want to see you in here again," Margaret called after me. The other addicts came over to me and wished me the best of luck. I stepped out of the ward into the real world again. Once more I looked calm on the outside but inside I was terrified. "Take me to Clontarf," I said to the taxi driver. "14 Mount Prospect Grove." I settled down for the ten-minute drive home. I lasted five minutes; then I told the taxi driver to take me to Fairview.

"Make your mind up," the driver said.

"Just take me to Fairview," I said. On arrival in Fairview I jumped out of the taxi and got some Valium in the chemist's. I immediately ran across the road to the park and took ten of them. I hadn't lasted half-an-hour; I was already back on drugs.

I promised myself that I wouldn't take any more. I knew of a Narcotics Anonymous meeting in Abbey Street in the city centre. I would go there tomorrow. I waited for the Valium to take effect and then I went home to my mother's house. I stayed in for the rest of the day. I reassured her that I was fine and that I was going to start going to NA and Alcoholics Anonymous. She was pleased I was making the effort to sort myself out.

The Marathon Man

That night my brother Michael came to visit me at my mother's. He was glad to see me. He had taken up running and he knew that I had had running ambitions at one time.

"Hey, John, do you think you could do the Dublin Marathon this year? You've got eight months left to train if you start now. What do you think?" I knew he was trying to encourage me in my effort to reform. I liked that about Michael – he was caring, and even though he was the youngest of the family he seemed to have an understanding of how I ticked.

"Michael, I think I'm too sick to do a m-marathon. Maybe I could do a 10 kilometre race in six months."

"You need to set your sights higher, John. I believe you could run a marathon. I'll even train you if you like." He was putting out a challenge to me and I enjoyed that. I thought about it for a minute.

"I'll give it a shot if you train me," I replied. "I'm not very w-well, Michael," I added. "My liver is not too good and I'm not sure if I can stay off drugs and drink."

"John, this would give you something to focus on. It would help you get fit and give you an incentive to stay off drugs and drink."

"OK," I said finally. "I *will* give it a shot. When do we start?"

"I'll come and get you tomorrow and we'll go up to St Anne's and start our training."

DEATH OF MY DAD

Next day Michael came for me at three in the afternoon. He walked me round the four-mile perimeter of St Anne's Estate. I managed it well enough. Bit by bit Michael trained me to run again. Within four months I was running nearly 60 miles a week, including a twenty-mile run on Sunday mornings. I got myself a job with the Irish Wheelchair Association as janitor. I was earning a regular wage and was going regularly to NA and AA meetings. Sometimes I fell back on drugs and drink, and of course my abuse of Valium continued – I needed to take at least ten to fifteen of them just to get by. I was still able to keep training and working though. I was doing my best. I raised £500 sponsorship for the Irish Wheelchair Association.

October came around; race day was on the 31st. I was excited but nervous. I took several Valium before going to run the race. Michael and his wife Denise met me and Michael gave me last-minute instructions on how to pace myself. The race was starting beside Merion Square on Dublin's south side. I got a good position and waited for the starting gun. At nine o'clock on the dot the gun went off and the huge crowd began to move forward. "Well, here I go," I thought. We quickened our pace from walking to running. I was feeling great; the atmosphere was electric. It was good to be alive. I passed the half-way thirteen-mile mark in 87 minutes; I was on course for my three-and-a-half-hour target. I felt good, like I was born to run. I just flowed for the whole race. The last two miles were tough but I finished the race in three hours, 26 minutes and 29 seconds. As soon as I had stopped running, I sat down and smoked about five cigarettes in a row to get the nicotine back into me. I was so proud of my achievement. Michael and Denise came to congratulate me.

"Well done, bro," he said, "you did it! I told you that you could, didn't I?" We went for something to eat and talked non-stop about the race. I believed in myself a bit more now than I had in years.

I slept like a log that night and the following day my legs were so sore that I had to come down the stairs of the house on my backside. I went for a little drink to celebrate my race victory that evening. "I will just have a few drinks, just for tonight," I told myself, "then I'll stop again." The next thing I knew it was several days later. I don't remember a thing about those few days. The £500 sponsorship money I had raised for the Irish Wheelchair Association was gone. I had spent the lot. I don't know where I stayed during that time; I took a complete blackout. I also lost my job. I had to borrow £500 from the Credit Union to pay the sponsorship money.

I was down-and-out again. I left my mother's house and stayed with friends till I got my own flat. I was too sick to work so I started to beg in Dublin, something I thought I would never do. "How is it that I sabotage every attempt to get my life together?" I wondered, feeling so disappointed in myself. I had just run a marathon, everything was going well; why had I messed everything up on myself again?

Yet I tried again, attending AA meetings every day, sometimes up to three times a day. I felt I had to somehow take control of my life. Several doctors offered me methadone, but I refused it.

I knew of many people who were on methadone courses. Methadone was a substitute for heroin and was being given out by the government to addicts who wanted or felt they needed it. Some of my friends began to believe that they had only one chance of getting off drugs and that was by going on methadone. I refused to take it because I believed that there was more freedom that could be experienced in life than that which methadone offered; I just hadn't achieved it yet. But I was beginning to run out of options.

I visited psychiatrists, some of whom seemed to be more screwed-up than me. My counsellors wanted me to sort my present out, by visiting the pain of my past and trying to discover the reasons I was addicted in the first place. I knew that there was some value in this because I had done it many times in my life. It had helped me come to terms with difficult issues, and talking about them had brought some healing to those areas. Yet I felt that there was something that needed to break, something deep down within me, a dark power that was at work to control me. I sometimes found myself walking into an off-licence or into a pub or into a pharmacist's shop or drug dealer's house against my will. I would often repeat to myself, "I don't want to go in here; I don't want this drink or drug" – yet I felt like there was a magnet pulling me into those places and there was nothing I could do to stop it. This addiction or pull towards drugs and drink was bigger than I was, and beyond my control.

My friends in Alcoholics Anonymous and Narcotics Anonymous talked about handing the care of your life over to God, as you understood Him, or a power greater than yourself. This power was mentioned particularly in the first three steps of the AA and NA programme. As I sat in on the meetings I noticed that the practice of talking about one's past was only encouraged *after* one had handed the care of one's life over to this higher power. They realised that a power encounter had to come first, and this made sense to me. I began to wonder how I could have this encounter. I struggled with the "God" bit; I was confused about who He was. On the one hand I felt that He wanted to punish me and give me a hard time, and on the other I had, on occasions, experienced some people talk about a God of love.

At this point, I would get a few weeks drink-free or drug-free. I never gave up the Valium completely; I was too afraid to stop using everything. I couldn't seem to take the decisive step away from them. I was afraid to, and during this time I fell back on the drugs again. I went on a huge binge of drink and drugs, I suffered many memory losses during my bingeing, this time I lost nearly two weeks of my life. I don't know where I went, what I did or how I survived. I came to myself one night in Dublin and hardly knew my name. I was dirty, smelly and very, very sick. I had taken a serious blackout.

I managed to make my way to a meeting of Alcoholics Anonymous in Killester in Dublin. It was a Sunday morning. A couple of people shared about an encounter they had had with God. A "spiritual awakening", they called it. I had a chat with them at the end of the meeting and they told me how God had helped them. They shared in a way that I, as a Catholic, could understand.

Chapter Seventeen
Help From On High

A Watershed in My Life

I observed these people for several months and got to know many of them – Ursula, Liam, Cathy, Mick . . . I realised that there was something these people had that I didn't have. I couldn't quite put my finger on what it was beyond an obvious peace and tranquillity. They had fun together, but there was something more, something different. I discovered that they went to a Christian meeting in the Howth Lodge, a hotel in the north side of Dublin. I decided to go with them.

The next meeting was scheduled for the third Wednesday of August 1987; when the day arrived I took my best clothes out, ironed them and got myself ready. I was very nervous about going. I wanted what they had but I was afraid that this spiritual awakening would not happen to me.

Maybe I was destined to be an addict all my life; maybe I should just go on methadone like most other addicts; maybe I was being foolish to think that there was a way out of this trap. Why would God help me, anyway? What had I ever done to deserve help from Him? I was probably being foolish to even think that God is real. What about evolution? Maybe that is reality; maybe I came from a monkey and addicts are just a mistake in evolution that needs to be medicated to survive – perhaps addiction was in my genes: after all, my father was, alcoholic. What about aliens? What about this and what about that?

I was in turmoil thinking of all the possibilities and all the impossibilities.

Half-past six came; it was time to catch my bus. If I was going to go, I'd better get a move on.

The bus pulled up outside the Howth Lodge at 7.15 p.m. I walked up the winding driveway to the front doors of this posh hotel. I found myself in the reception area. I was nervous, feeling very insecure and vulnerable.

"Excuse me," I asked the receptionist, "c-can you tell me where the C-Christian meeting is on?"

"Do you mean the Full Gospel meeting?" the receptionist asked.

"I guess so."

"Just go up the stairs and go into the big room at the top and that is where it is on."

"Thank you," I replied as I turned to go up the stairs. Liam and Cathy saw me enter the big room.

"Hey, John – come and join us." They beckoned me to their table. Ursula was there also. I knew I could relax with them. We had a nice evening together, enjoying a chicken and ham dinner with coffee afterwards. Once the meal was finished and the staff had cleared the dishes away a man called Barry got up with a guitar and sang some lovely Christian songs. Everybody joined in and clapped their hands. I was very self-conscious and was slow to join in with them. Then some guy told his story about how God had saved him and changed his life. I did not have a spiritual awakening that night but I did enjoy the evening. I had only one regret and that was that my self-consciousness had stopped me from joining in with the singing.

The meeting finished at about 9.30 p.m. Liam gave me a lift home afterwards. "Well, John, we have another meeting the third Wednesday in September if you want to come."

"Thanks, Liam, I will. I really enjoyed the evening."

"Remember, John," Liam replied, "God has a wonderful plan for your life."

That night I lay awake thinking about the meeting. I had not only enjoyed it but had also felt a peace there that I had felt before – it was a bit like the peace I had experienced when I used to visit the "Children of God" as a teenager. I could see that the people at the meeting had something that I needed. I would go to the next meeting . . .. I thought about Liam's statement that God has a wonderful plan for my life. I wanted to believe it but it sounded too good to be true. Yet I held on to that promise in my heart.

The weeks seemed to go past very slowly but at last the third Wednesday of September came along. Once again I dressed myself up as best I could and got the bus to the Howth Lodge Hotel. I found myself sitting with a few strangers that night. They were friendly and we chatted over the meal. When the meal was over I went to the back of the big room and stood by myself waiting for Barry to start singing like he had on the previous occasion. The lights were low, everyone was looking towards the front of the room and I was standing with my back against the wall. I made sure that nobody could see me or was watching me. I wanted to sing those hymns and I wanted to mean what they said.

God Really Is There

Somebody had given me a song-book earlier and I was full of anticipation as Barry stood up with his guitar to sing. He gave the number of the song in the book and began to sing. I turned to the page and nervously started to sing along. The words were lovely. They spoke about a God who loved us unconditionally, who never gave up on us, a God who knew us intimately; who knew all our problems and wanted to set us free. I so much wanted to believe that God was like these words said. I needed God if He was really there to touch my life and change me. I stopped singing and started praying. "God – if you are the God that these lovely words say you are; if you can be personal to me and change me, if you can set me free from the horrible pain and addiction I have carried around for most of my life – then please help me." I then added, "God, I will put down the drugs and the drink but if you are real then please be real to me. I don't want to follow something that is not real. You need to be so real to me that I can feel your presence every day." I was crying now and pleading with God to come and reveal Himself to me.

The other people at the meeting were totally unaware of what was going on at the back of the room between God and myself. For the first time in my adult life I was genuinely asking God for help. I began again to sing along; we were repeating the word "Alleluia, Alleluia". I didn't know what it meant but I expressed my heart to God through that worship song. I found out afterwards that Alleluia means "Praise You Lord". I began to feel as if something was happening. I was not sure what, but peace was beginning to flood my mind and body.

Suddenly, unexpectedly – it was as if the roof of the building burst off and the very hand of God came in and touched me on the top of my head. I could feel His power shooting straight down my body and something very evil leaving me. It felt as if a steel cord or belt had snapped on the inside of my belly. Then once again this incredible power flooded through me. I began to shake all over. The feeling was stronger than any drug, drink or any other experience I had ever had. God was touching my life and He had become real to me!

People began to notice that something was happening and a girl approached me. Her name was Ann Reynolds, Barry's wife. She got a chair for me and told me to sit down before I fell down. "What is your name?" she asked me.

"John Edwards," I replied.

"Well, John Edwards," she said, "I don't know what your background is but I can tell you whatever it is, God has just come into your life and you will never be the same again."

Liam, Cathy, Ursula, her brother Allan and his wife Jean came over to me and said that I had just had a spiritual awakening; Jesus Christ had come into a personal relationship with me. I felt completely clean, forgiven and so very happy. I had never felt so happy in my life before. It was as if God had just shown me that He is greater than any drug or drink: He is the Most High.

Ellis Rowland was the main leader of the Full Gospel meeting and he introduced himself to me. He then introduced me to some others who would play an important part in my life over the next few years; people like Paddy Keegan and his wife Pauline, Pat and Patricia McGrath, Eddie and Margaret and old

Tom. They gave me a Bible and taught me the word of God. I loved reading the Bible; it seemed to come alive for me. I read through the entire New Testament several times during the next few months. Ellis and his wife Marie introduced me to St Mark's Church on Pearse Street in Dublin's city centre. This was a very lively church. The worship music was beautiful and the people were very friendly. I loved it there and I made many friends. The pastor, Gary Davidson, was a great preacher. I had never heard anyone talk about the Bible in such a way. It was relevant to the twentieth century, it was a handbook, a compass, a guidebook to help us through the world and steer us safely through all the pitfalls and snares of life.

I lived on this new experience for a few months, but I was still addicted to Valium. Every day I would have to go out and get my drugs. I always felt so guilty doing this and when I had my drugs in me I would ask God to forgive me. I was getting to know Him and I knew that He accepted me as I was. Unfortunately I sometimes caused a lot of trouble when I fell back on drugs. On one particular night I was stoned out of my head on a mixture of drugs and drink. I was with two neighbours of mine. Suddenly I remembered that the Full Gospel meeting was on at the Howth Lodge; I insisted that they both come along with me to the meeting. I wouldn't take no for an answer.

When we arrived, I sat at the back of the room and fell into a drugged, drunken stupor. The speaker offered to pray for people at the end of the meeting. My two neighbours took hold of me, lifted me by my arms and led me down between the tables towards the front. There were about sixty people there in total. Then the speaker who had offered to pray for people came towards me. He put his hands out to touch me. I don't know what I was thinking at the time – perhaps I thought he was going to hit me – but the last thing I remember is kicking him as hard as I could between the legs. I saw him fall like a sack of potatoes. I don't remember a thing after that, but it seems that I lost complete control of myself then. Several of the leaders of the meeting jumped on me and tried to get me out by the fire exit. I'm told that I tried to throw two of them over the first-floor railings of the fire escape. They managed to lock me out but I then ran around the front of the hotel, in through the front door and up the stairs to the meeting-room. They had anticipated me coming and had locked the paned glass door that led to the room. I then proceeded to kick a way through the panes of glass and severed a vein in my left leg as I scrambled into the room. It looked as if all hell had broken loose, with women screaming and men running everywhere. They said I seemed to have superhuman strength and that I was foaming at the mouth before I collapsed in a heap. They called an ambulance and I was brought to a Dublin hospital.

I can remember nothing of the entire episode from the time I kicked the man until I awoke in the hospital. I didn't know where I was. Ellis Rowland, Paddy Keegan, Pat McGrath and others were sitting around the bed. "Where am I?" I asked. "What are you all doing here?"

They told me all about the night before. I was horrified, mortified – how could I have done such a thing? I tried to apologise, but I was so ashamed of myself that I was at a loss for words.

"John," Ellis said, "the main reason that we are here is that we want you to know that we are going to stick with you. We forgive you for what happened last night. We see your potential. We believe that you can put all this behind you and be a success, one day. We are convinced that God has great plans for your life and we're not about to give up on you. God loves you, John, and so do we."

I had only ever seen love like this in my Salvation Army friends, David and Lorraine; no one else had ever had that kind of faith in me. I was very ashamed at what had happened but I felt supported by these men. I was amazed at their faith in me.

Pat McGrath visited me many times in my flat. He would come round to encourage me and bless me in whatever way he could. I attended the Monday night meeting where these men prayed and planned the gospel dinners. I am sure they sometimes groaned when they saw me coming.

I pulled myself together as best I could and soon managed to get a flat at 77 Clontarf Road, where the landlord was a family friend. He knew me and yet he gave me one of his flats! I was struggling once again with drugs and drink. One night I was reading the Bible in my flat, feeling desperate about my addiction. I called out to God for help. "Lord," I prayed, "I need you to be real to me, to help me get beyond my addiction. I am powerless on my own – please help me." I fell on my knees, placed the Bible on a chair in front of me and lifted my hands into the air as a sign of my surrender. "God, I do not know what to do. I know you are real so I worship you and trust you, Father." Suddenly, as I said, "I worship you. Father." I sensed the presence of God in the room. I said again, "I worship you, Father." Again, the presence of God came washing like a wave over me. I continued praying like this for a few minutes and suddenly there was the appearance of what looked like light or liquid ice in the corner of my little one-room bed-sit. I was transfixed; I couldn't talk, move or do anything, the sense of holiness and love was so overwhelming. I was caught up in the presence of God, experiencing the reality of the presence of the Person of the Holy Spirit. God was visiting me. I remained lost in His presence for several hours and then I fell asleep.

Next morning was a Sunday. I woke up and I was still filled with an overwhelming sense of the presence of God. I walked or rather floated into church that morning. I was heading towards my usual seat in St Mark's when one of the elders' wives came running over to me. "John, I can see the presence of the Holy Spirit all over you! What has happened? Your eyes are shining and there's an awesome aura about you." She then asked me to pray for her.

"What do you mean, 'pray for you'?" I asked. "Do you mean right here, right now?"

"Yes – lay your hands on my head and pray for me."

I felt a little self-conscious but I had read in the Bible that this was a way of praying for the sick. I reached out and as I touched her head she suddenly shot back as if a bolt of lightning had hit her. She slid on her back along the shiny floor of St Mark's for about ten feet. I felt, ironically, both shocked and unsurprised. I knew that the power of God was flowing through me.

This beautiful sense of His presence stayed with me until the Wednesday. Four glorious days caught up in God's presence! It is an experience I will never ever forget, although it was not to be the last by any means.

I began to attend a prayer meeting in Coolock in Dublin. Charlie and Marie Protheroe held a meeting in their home every Tuesday evening. Barry Reynolds was the worship leader here too. He was also a great Bible teacher. I began to bring some friends along, including my best pal at the time, a guy called Paul Sunderland. As he attended the meetings he too had a wonderful experience with God.

One night I had a dream that I was in a big American car driving through a familiar part of Dublin. In this dream many young people were lining the streets and crying out for help. I was seated in the back seat of the car and I was filled with compassion for these people. I opened the door and began to pull many of them into the car. I knew that once they were in the car they were safe. I then awoke, and felt sure that the dream had prophetic significance. Time would tell.

God's provision for me was becoming evident in little practical matters. At around this time I started looking for a bigger flat, as I had got myself a German Shepherd dog and I needed more room for him. As time passed I had been given a bed, a three-piece suite, linen, towels, knives, forks, spoons, plates, cups, saucers, a stereo, a television and everything else I needed for a flat but I still had not found the flat itself. Then one Tuesday night at the prayer meeting I was told there was a flat available for rent in Fairview, a part of Dublin I had not lived in before. I viewed the flat and it was perfect for me. It was unfurnished so all the furniture I had been given fitted perfectly into it. I settled in nicely and very soon my pals began to call around. The guy who lived upstairs was a Christian; he used to come down to my flat for a chat most evenings, and soon another tenant at the back of the house became a Christian also. Another lad living just down the road began to bring his guitar around most nights. He soon became a Christian and he learnt some lovely Christian hymns that he sang for us in the evenings. Jimmy, the owner of the little corner shop across the road, heard about our Christian gatherings and he began to tell his customers about it. In no time at all many of his customers were coming for prayer to my flat.

One night my old fighting partner, Bob, who had chopped my ear in half, came into the flat. "Johnny, does your God heal?" he asked me.

"Yes," I answered.

"Well, can he heal my arm?"

I knew that Bob's arm had not worked properly since he was thirteen. He had fallen off his bike and it had frozen at the elbow. He could only bend it a couple of inches. Bob and I had never been the same friends since that night in the bus shelter when he almost killed me. "Why should I pray for him?" I thought to myself, " and even if I do, will God do anything?" I prayed silently, "God, do you want me to pray for him?" Of course, I didn't hear a voice speak back but I did feel at peace about praying.

"Right, Bob, take off your jacket," I said. "I will pray for you and I believe that God can heal you. When I pray don't stop me. You might not have faith, but I do." Bob looked a little startled at my reply, but he did as I had asked him. I sat him down in a chair and rolled up his sleeve; then, putting my hand on his elbow, I began praying.

"In Jesus' name, be healed," I said. Immediately the whole area around his elbow began to pulsate. Bob was shocked. I took hold of his wrist and bent his arm up. To Bob's surprise and my joy, his arm bent up for the first time in over twenty years. Bob was amazed. He told many people about the healing that God had done for him. As word got around, many more people began to call in. Single mothers came and asked me to pray for their babies, alcoholics, drug addicts, the sick, the homeless and even the local priest, Father Gerald. They all, including Father Gerald, had an experience with God. He became real to them; He met them at their point of need and saved them. In total over 100 people came through that flat in the year I lived there. Some went on to Bible College; others attended St Mark's or other churches around Dublin.

I was thinking about all this one day when I remembered the dream I had had about my going through Dublin in the big black car. The street that that car was going down in the dream was the street that my flat was on and the people who had been coming to the meetings all lived there. I was amazed when I realised this.

Yet in spite of all that, I knew that I needed further help in my life. From time to time I was still falling back on drugs and drink and many Christians accused me of being a hypocrite. I knew better than anyone just how much I fell short of what I believed God wanted for my life. Some said I couldn't be a Christian, others said that I was a hopeless case and that I would never get my life together. Yet even in the midst of all this, God's presence never left me. I decided to leave Dublin and go to Bible College in Galway, if they would have me.

A Yo-Yo Life

I arranged to go to hospital for another detox. It took me six weeks; this time when I came out I managed to stay clean long enough to have an interview for Bible College. My friend Paul drove me to Galway. I was very nervous meeting the college pastor and head teacher, Graeme Wiley, but he was a lovely man and he accepted me for enrolment. In September I returned to live in Galway, leaving my dog in the care of a friend. I shared a house in Tirellan Heights just outside Galway City.

I settled in well and began my studies. Most of the others in the class were younger and more used to studying than I. I found the pressure of trying to control my addiction along with my efforts to study extremely difficult. Eventually I asked Graeme to allow me drop some of the classes. Much to my relief he agreed.

While living in Galway I had barely enough to live on. One day I ran out of milk and I had no money to buy any. This upset me, as I was not due any money for nearly a week. I prayed that day and asked God to help me financially. I felt it was a bit cheeky to ask such a thing but I had always asked God to be real to me. That night I shared with some of my friends in college about my financial position. All of them were going through similar difficulties, so we arranged to meet in one of their houses to pray. About ten of us gathered and we stormed heaven with prayer for about an hour. Then we went on home. We truly believed that God had heard us.

The very next day, when I arrived in Bible College, Graeme gave me a brown envelope. "This was left on my desk for you, John," he said. I took the envelope and put it into my bag. I thought it contained some form to apply for one of the college examinations, or something like that, and I put it out of my mind as I began studying. Later in the afternoon, during a coffee break, I remembered the envelope. I took it out and opened it. To my great surprise it contained a gift cheque. There was no name on it, so I could not tell who it came from, but on the cover of the gift cheque there was a verse of scripture, Philippians 4:19: "My God shall supply all your need according to His glorious riches in Christ Jesus." The amount was for £350 and 28 pence. I was so excited that I ran straight off to the home of one of the other students who had prayed, wanting to share the good news about the answer to prayer. To my amazement, he told me that he too had received a cheque for the same amount. We immediately called to see our other pals who had prayed and sure enough, each of the ten of us had received a gift cheque for the same amount. There was no name on the cheques, just an initial that could not be deciphered. Each cheque had a scripture verse on it reminding us of the promise of God's provision.

During my stay in Galway I experienced God performing fantastic miracles, including people being healed on the streets. On one occasion, I got to share my life story for the first time with travellers who had been settled in houses in Lochrae, a small town in another part of the county. Seven of them became Christians that night. In October I got baptised in a freezing-cold lake with several gypsies and a couple of my friends from the college.

Yet I was still struggling with my studies, and my nerves were clearly shattered from the years of drug-taking. One night I felt particularly desperate so I went to a doctor for a prescription for Valium. After taking them I got very drunk and took another blackout.

Chapter Eighteen
Hitting Rock Bottom

I regained consciousness in a part of Galway that I didn't recognise. It was a bitterly cold; I was wet right through to my skin and shaking like a leaf from the cold and from withdrawals. I needed to find somewhere to sleep, and quickly. As I walked I came across a gypsy camp. "Maybe I'll find help here," I thought, and approached one of the caravans. Anxiously I knocked on the door, but there was no answer. I tried another and again there was no answer. Perhaps they were all sleeping. I was getting desperate; the cold was beginning to creep into my bones. I was shivering uncontrollably. I had to find somewhere dry or else I would freeze. Suddenly I noticed a horsebox behind one of the caravans. I walked around to it quietly, and pulling the door of the horsebox back slowly, I peered in through the opening. It was pitch-dark inside but as my eyes adjusted to the dark I began to make out the shape of a huge grey Shire horse standing looking at me. He was massive, about eighteen hands in height. The horse didn't get upset at me and I slipped into the box, hoping that he would not react or make a lot of noise. He began to shift and make snorting sounds, so I responded by singing a hymn; it may sound crazy but it was all I could think of to do. Strangely, the horse calmed right down. I carefully and slowly approached him and put my arms round his neck to get some of his heat into me. He didn't budge but stayed very calm. I remained like this till I had warmed up a bit; then I closed the door of the horsebox tight to keep out the wind. I then gathered up some of his straw and put it in the holes and cracks of the door where the wind was still getting through. I pulled some more of the straw into a pile that I could lie on. It smelled of horse dung and urine but I was in survival mode and I had to make the best of it. I didn't know any other way. I peeled off my wet jacket and jumper and wrung the water out of them. Then I lay down in the straw using the wet jumper as a pillow and covering myself with the wet jacket. I had to survive the night.

Rock Bottom

I couldn't sleep; I was freezing and my head felt like a bomb had gone off in it. I had no drink, no drugs, and no human being to help me or even to talk to me. I felt extremely lonely and I was crying again, something I seemed to be doing a lot of during those days. But my cries now were more desperate – far more desperate than ever before. The horse bent down his head and nudged me gently, as if saying, "You're not alone." His breath was smelly but warm and therefore welcome.

"When is this craziness going to stop?" I cried. "When is it going to stop?"

I began to think of the prodigal son in the Bible story; he had squandered his inheritance and didn't come to his senses until he was living in a pigpen and eating out of the pigs' trough. His father met him with open arms when he returned and put a party on for him. I wondered if God would accept me back if I returned to church and got some help. Survival instinct and a search for meaning in my miserable existence kicked into play. I thought over my life: the dead friends, the mental institutions, living on the streets of London, all the rejection, abuse, overdosing, comas, fights and near-death experiences. What a waste if I were to die now. The horse kept nudging me and blowing warm breath over my face and body. He was so gentle, as if he knew to respect this moment in my life. I dozed for a while, waking now and then as the horse nudged me. I had never felt so low before in my life. I had been in more dangerous situations; I had been colder, I had been more essentially homeless. This time, though, something happened inside me. I went down as low as I had ever been. I sank to deep darkness. I experienced my dark night of the soul, my rock bottom. I had almost given up; everything seemed to be without hope. I stayed with this feeling for a long time: I didn't even fight it now, I was beaten. I had never been completely beaten before, but now, here, in this horsebox, I was beaten. I had no more solutions, no more escapes or ideas. I lay there freezing, a shivering mess, defeated.

Slowly the day began to dawn. Light began to penetrate the darkness of the stable. I turned round to look up at the horse; he was looking down at me.

"Hey!" I said aloud, "the sun is rising again and I don't have the strength to face another day like this. I'm feeling very old and I haven't got any recoveries left in me. I'm beaten." I reached up to the big horse, stroked his nose and said, "You're the only witness to the final round in this fight, horse. I don't even have hope left, except hope that maybe God can do something – a miracle."

The day was getting brighter; I rolled over, reached out my hand to push open the door of the horsebox and looked out. It was a grey, drizzly, cold morning, a reflection of how I felt. I turned back into my stable again and looked up at the horse. I felt convinced that he was looking directly at me as if he were keeping guard over me. I reached up my hand and touched the front of his head. " Horse," I said, "I can't go any lower without dying; I can't fight any more – so I'm giving in and going for some long-term help. This is my last chance and I'll give it all I've got. If that doesn't work then I may as well just die."

I pulled myself to my feet; I was very stiff and cold to the bones. I put my arms around the horse again to get some heat and then exited the horsebox. "Bye, horse, thanks for the bed for the night." I stepped out of the horsebox into the grey light of an unknown future, yet in spite of the uncertainty I somehow knew that things were going to be different.

"Hey, what are you doing in there?" a voice called out to me. It was one of the gypsies.

"I got lost last night and I had nowhere to sleep so I stayed in the horsebox," I replied.

"What!" he exclaimed, and he appeared shocked. "You're lucky to be alive. That horse is a mad one – that's the reason he's in the box; all the other horses are in the field over here" and he pointed to where some horses were grazing together. "You're one blessed man, whoever you are," he continued. "That horse could have killed you."

I walked into Galway city, calling in to a house belonging to two of my friends for a shower on the way.

"John, you look terrible," Des and Ros said, "and you stink of horse dung."

"Phone Graeme Wiley for me, w-will you, Des?" I answered. "I'm going home to get h-help. I can't live like this any more. I'm leaving today." I explained everything that had happened and the decision I had made to go away and get some proper help.

I had the shower and Des gave me some clean clothes. By the time I was back downstairs Graeme and his wife Fran were waiting for me. I explained the situation to them and they agreed that it was best that I leave the Bible College and get help for my problems.

Most of the other students came to see me then and they prayed with me and encouraged me. Graeme gave me the money for a bus ticket to Dublin and before evening I was on my way home.

I didn't hang around for long in Dublin, although I did get some Valium to help me through the days ahead. I took about fifteen to twenty a day. My friends Alan and Jean Coyle gave me a room in their lovely house. I gave away all my earthly belongings except my clothes and went off to Belfast to be interviewed for a place in a Christian rehabilitation centre called "Teen Challenge" in South Wales. The man who interviewed me was a former terrorist named David Hamilton. David had a tremendous testimony of how God had changed the direction of his life. He gave me a lot of hope and told me that God had great plans for me.

Within a week, word came through that I was accepted for the Teen Challenge programme and I was on the waiting list. I had to wait six weeks before a place was available for me. My friend Jean got sick during that time, so Alan asked me if I could help around the house while she was in hospital. I agreed and spent the next few weeks looking after Sarah, Niamh, Aisling and Ian. My hands were full. Here I was, sick and tired of life, barely hanging in there – and now I had to look after the house and kids for my friends–! I thought that I would not be able to manage it, but as it turned out I think I did quite well. Alan, Jean and their family gave me hope, a huge welcome and unconditional love. They were, and are, like a second family to me. Sadly Jean has since died. She was such a lovely girl and a good friend, a sad loss to us all. I would not have survived during those six weeks had she and Alan not been there for me.

Chapter Nineteen
I've Only One
Recovery Left in Me

Back to Britain

I received a phone call from Teen Challenge on the 6th April 1991. A man called Mike Rankin told me that a place was available for me to attend their programme. He gave me a list of things I needed to bring with me and told me to be there by 10th April.

Alan and Jean and the kids were delighted for me when they heard the good news. Yet I think that the kids were sad to see me go and I was sorry to leave them, as I had grown very close to them.

That Sunday in St Marks I told Gary Davidson, the pastor, that I had been accepted in Teen Challenge and that I would be leaving in a couple of days. He was delighted for me but at the same time he told me to commit myself to completing the course. "You are the first Irish guy to go to Teen Challenge, John; make sure that you do well and never go back on drugs or drink again."

"I will do it, Gary," I replied. "I'm determined to finish the programme." He hugged me and prayed for me. St Mark's helped me with the fare for my ticket, as I had spent nearly all my money on the kids. All my friends in the church said their goodbyes to me and wished me well as I left: Shay, Brian, Ann, Denise, Peter, Anna, Gary's wife Wilma, my pals Paul and Des, Pat and many, many more. I had never had so many friends in my life before. I had all these great people to come back to.

WALKING FREE

I didn't want to tell my family that I was going to a rehab again; they had heard it all before, so I told them that I was going to work in Wales at a Christian centre. They were happy for me, and somewhat relieved, I suppose.

I said my goodbyes to Alan and Jean and the kids, and to Jean's sister Pauline. Some of their neighbours came in to say goodbye as well. It really was quite upsetting parting with everyone, but at last I was out of Dublin and heading for Rosslare to catch the boat that would take me to South Wales.

Before getting on the boat I took my last twenty Valium tablets and a can of Guinness. This would keep me going, at least until I got there. I found a seat in a quiet part of the boat and read my Bible as I travelled to Wales. I desperately wanted this to be the last boat trip I would make as an addict. I didn't take any alcohol on the boat; I was determined to stop everything before I got to the centre. When I disembarked I took the train from Fishguard to Swansea. I phoned Teen Challenge from the railway station to let them know that I had arrived and then bought myself a cup of tea to wait for them to come and collect me.

I was ready to put my past behind me at last. "This is it," I thought, "I either make it this time or I'm finished." I had tried everything to get my life together and so far nothing had worked. Psychiatrists, counsellors, secular rehabilitation centres, mental institutions, detox programmes, six-week programmes, ten-week programmes, going to live in foreign countries, methadone courses – none of these had worked. I had even tried a "God cure"; whenever a new preacher, evangelist or Bible teacher would come into town I would go to him, sometimes travelling over 100 miles to be there. I would ask them to pray for me. Some of them told me to throw my drugs and drink away, for I was now healed. "Fantastic," I thought; "I will now give them my drugs and that will be it." I gave my drugs to so-called preachers like this many times only to wake up sick the next day. Some said that I didn't have faith, so I went without my drugs on one occasion for two weeks only to endure fits and terrible suffering. I was looking for the simple, instant answer to my problems but it was not to happen, not to me anyway.

I'VE ONLY ONE RECOVERY LEFT IN ME

Now here I was, within minutes from entering a Christian rehabilitation programme, asking a God that I could not see to set me free from my addictions and from the past with all its hurts, pains and abuses. It seemed somewhat ironic; I had tried everything that man could dream up to get my life together – now I was going into a programme where I had to believe that a power greater than myself, a God whom I could not see, would set me free. The beautiful thing about it was that I was surer than I had ever been before that I could make it now with God's help.

I pulled furiously on my last roll-up cigarette and finished my tea. I could see a man in a woolly blue jumper walking towards me and I guessed that he was the man from Teen Challenge. I took one deep, final pull on the roll-up; I nearly gave myself a hernia I pulled so hard on it. I had been smoking continually for 24 years but this was it, I was giving up everything. I threw the roll-up on the ground and crushed it almost to dust under my foot. Then I quietly prayed, "Lord, into your hands I commit my life. Please set me free."

"Hello! Are you John Edwards?"

"I am," I answered.

"My name is Roy. It's good to meet you. Welcome to Teen Challenge. The car is waiting outside." Picking up the small bag that contained all my earthly belongings he said, "Is this all you have?"

"Yes," I answered, embarrassed. He could see that I was a bit nervous, so he chatted to me about the programme and put me at ease during the twenty-minute drive to the centre.

We drove into a little Welsh village called Gorslas, where the centre was situated. There were sixteen other men on the programme. They gave me a warm welcome. The building itself was painted a light yellow on the outside; it was like a rabbit warren, with corridors everywhere. I was shown around the building and given a bed in a double room. "You are in here on your own tonight, John. Your new room-mate is arriving from Scotland tomorrow. His name is Gerry Rankin. He is about the same age as yourself so you should get on well."

"Thanks, Roy."

Roy left me on my own to settle into my room. There was a dead plant on the high windowsill; I took it down and looked closely at it. The soil was completely dry and there was no sign of it recovering. "That is just like me," I thought. "I'll water it and see if it will come alive." I put water in it and loosed the soil around the top of the pot to allow the water go to its roots. I then did what may seem like a silly thing: I prayed for it to recover and put it back on the windowsill. I put my toothbrush in its place by the sink in the room and then I went downstairs. I did another silly thing on the way down the stairs; I put my index finger through the wallpaper at the corner where the paper had bubbled a bit and where it would not be noticed. I then promised myself that I would look at that little hole on the day I completed the programme.

I was introduced to the rest of the staff later in the day; John Macey, the founder and director, his wife Ann, Pastor Hughes and his wife Margot, and John Macey's secretary, Audrey, who was Mike Rankin's wife. Audrey was an amazing girl, full of life and fun and she was a great encouragement to us all. She helped make the centre what it was. Then I met Gareth Cheedy, who was to be my counsellor. He played a huge part in my recovery. Next there was the centre handyman Roy, the resident fixer of all things and another great encouragement. Another staff member was Finley Moffat, along with his wife Christine. Finley had been an addict himself. Finally there was Shirley and "Mrs A", the cooks – and of course, Nancy, the woman who washed our clothes. Without her the centre would have stopped running. Well, it may have kept running but it would have been very smelly . . .

I slept fairly well the first night, and on the following morning, instead of feeling the withdrawals from Valium kicking in, I felt strangely okay.

The year of the Teen Challenge programme was the quickest and happiest year of my life up to that time. I hardly suffered any withdrawals from drugs. I was set free from cigarettes, drink and drugs on that same day, 10th April 1991.

I'VE ONLY ONE RECOVERY LEFT IN ME

I loved the studies that we did: they were so practical. Among other things, they taught us how to love and accept ourselves, how to grow through failure and how to deal with anger issues. There were fourteen studies in all. I memorised verses of scripture, and the practical steps I should take when going through difficult times. The Bible seemed to open up to me and I felt as if God was speaking to me personally the whole way through the programme. I heard some students say that the programme was too hard or that they should be allowed to smoke or go out on their own or do this or that. There were always some that didn't take their time in Teen Challenge as seriously as they should. Many of these are dead today. The rest of them are like the walking dead, waiting to die.

I faced all my problems of hurt, pain and abuse bit by bit. I talked them through and prayed them through. Every day I would get on my knees and ask the Holy Spirit to help me and to set me free from the effects of my past. Everyone on the programme went through at least one serious testing. My main one came when I volunteered to get a blood test done. I had convinced myself that I was HIV positive because some of my friends in Dublin were dying from AIDS. I had shared needles with many of them so there was a good chance of my having the virus. I also could have caught it by sexual transmission.

I worried myself sick while I waited the two weeks for the results. I had to focus myself by praying and believing that everything would be okay. One day in particular I was wrestling with fear for my future regarding the HIV issue. I went into the little chapel in the centre, which was the only place I could get on my own. I needed to have a serious talk with God. I got down on my knees behind the drum kit so that no one could see me. I prayed more earnestly than I had since I came into the programme. "God," I prayed, "I always asked you to be real to me; now more than ever please be real to me. I ask you please to not let me have the AIDS virus. Please, God, not after all that I have been through . . ." I must have prayed like this for ten to fifteen minutes when suddenly a holy presence filled the little chapel where I knelt. I heard a voice speak to me; it was not a voice that I could hear with my ears but an inner one. Yet it was somehow clearer than an audible voice and it spoke right into my life.

" John," the voice said, "I thought that you had given your life to me?"

I began to weep as I felt the awesome presence of God. "I did give my life to you, God," I answered.

"If you gave your life to me, John, why are you so worried?"

"Lord," I said, "I have given everything up: drugs, drink, cigarettes, my family, my flat, everything I have ever owned I have given up to come here."

The voice then said a life-changing thing to me. "John, If you expect me to make you into the person that you want to be and into the person that I want you to be, you will have to give me your very self."

"I don't know how to, God," I answered.

"Surrender yourself to me; yield to me and I will take you from where you are to freedom."

I fell face down on the floor in the little chapel and the sweet presence of God swept over me for the next ten minutes. I cannot explain in ordinary words exactly what took place that day but I know that when I got up from the floor I was not the same. Something had happened. I didn't worry from that moment on whether I was HIV positive or not. It was like I was no longer living, but God was living in me – as though a resurrection life had taken over.

Everyone I knew in Teen Challenge that made it went through a tough time until they broke through before God. You can ask any man or woman who has made it from addiction to freedom in the Christian way and they will tell you that they broke before God before they were truly free.

I noticed a marked change in my life from that moment. I wanted to serve God now and I stopped worrying about going back on drugs or drink. I began to plan for my future. And thankfully, the results of my AIDS test were negative.

I started to train again. I ran every week on the running track in a nearby town called Carmarthen. I felt so good; I was fit and I was free of drugs, drink and cigarettes for the first time in nearly 24 years. Often I would be out running, flowing round

I'VE ONLY ONE RECOVERY LEFT IN ME

the 400 metre track with ease, tears streaming down my face in gratitude. "Oh thank you so much, Jesus, for setting me free; I am so grateful." It was so good to be alive, I was laughing again and I had real joy in my heart. The pain was over, the struggle to get free was gone; God had done something that man could not do for me. Jesus Christ had set me free.

When I was about six months into the programme I began to feel a desire to help people who suffered in the same way as I had. I wanted to go through Ireland and other parts of the world and proclaim to those held captive that Jesus wants to and will set them free if they will let Him. I wanted first to help addicts in my own country who were still suffering by praying for them.

I spent all my energy applying myself to the programme and by doing this I sailed through. There were times of pain, times for crying, times for crying out to God for help – but through it all I kept focused. There was no way I was going back to my past. I was hungry for God, for as much of God as I could get. I devoured the Bible and any other Christian books that I could get my hands on. I spent hours in the little library on the upstairs landing reading and learning from some of the great Christian scholars that had lived many years before. I studied doctrine until it was coming out of my ears. I always kept my Bible with me and read it on every occasion I could.

I watered my little plant in the room and it flourished as I flourished. Gerry my room-mate and I became great friends. He had four children back home in Inverness. He helped me water and care for the plant; it had lovely, free leaves and smelled of lemon. I do not know what kind it was but I called it my miracle tree.

The year-long programme was coming to an end. I was now allowed to have visits out for weekends. I made friends with Barry and Pauline Cundill and their children, a lovely Christian family who lived in Swansea. They took me home to stay with them for weekends and I felt really strange being out without drugs, drink or cigarettes. I was a different person; I thought different, I felt different, I even looked different – I *was* different. I was walking past chemist shops without having an urge to go in and try to get drugs. It felt great to be free.

WALKING FREE

Through Barry and Pauline and their lovely family I met many more people who played a positive role in my life. There were David and Beryl Ware, a truly special couple, so loving and kind to me. I learned so much from them. I can also remember Ivy, an older lady, and Mr Hugh Black, who became spiritual mentors to me and from whom I also learned a lot.

I joined the Teen Challenge Band, "The Evidence" and travelled around Britain with them. I mixed the sound for the band and I began to tell my life story publicly. Many people were touched by it. I felt privileged. My past was now beginning to work for me. What once disqualified me from many things in life was now, in a sense, beginning to qualify me for many things. That is the work of God.

Something unexpected began to happen to me on the programme. I was beginning to lose the stutter that I had struggled with all my life. I had learned to cope with it during the years but it had never completely gone. Now as my personality matured my handwriting began to straighten up; as I felt free to write the way a left-handed person should write, my stutter was completely healed. My father's efforts to make me write with my right hand had caused me to develop a stutter, but now my writing like a left-handed person had the opposite result. This was wonderful. All the effects of my past were going one by one.

April 1992 came along and my graduation day arrived. I was to be the first Irish man to graduate from the Teen Challenge Programme. On the day of my graduation I watered my miracle plant and then went to the stairs and put my finger into the hole that I had made in the wallpaper over a year before. "I've done it," I said. "I have completed something for the first time in my life." I enjoyed a great sense of personal triumph and silently thanked God for setting me free before I left for the celebration.

My friends Brian and Ann Kelly were the only people able to make it to the graduation from Ireland. I was a bit sad about this. "Well," I said to myself, "I am the first, a pioneer, breaking through for others. Things will be different for the next ones coming over."

The service was special. I received a graduation certificate.

I'VE ONLY ONE RECOVERY LEFT IN ME

On it are the words, "This is to certify that Mr John Edwards has successfully completed the course of Biblical studies in Teen Challenge Wales." I felt so proud, so happy that at last I had achieved freedom and completed the Teen Challenge course. This moment was so special to me, probably one of the most special moments in my entire life. Things could only get better from now on. I was shown lots of attention and given a big handclap. Many came up to me and congratulated me and afterwards we went for a lovely Indian meal in Ammanford, a local town.

Home to See My Ma

I travelled home the morning after my graduation service. I was looking forward to seeing my friends and family in Dublin now that I had completed the programme. I went straight to my mother's house. I didn't have to feel guilty this time; I was not stoned or drunk but was looking fit and well. I could hold my head high. I knocked on the door and waited. I had butterflies in my tummy; I couldn't wait to see her face. "Pull yourself together, John – you're like a kid," I told myself. Through the glass I could see her coming to open the door. I cleared my throat and brushed my hair back in anticipation of our embrace. The door opened and there stood my mam. She was getting old now but that day her big smile made her look youthful.

"Ah, John," she said. "It's so good to see you."

"Hiya, ma," I said as I reached out to give her a big hug. Tears filled my ma's eyes and ran down her face. I couldn't love anyone more than my ma at that moment. I had caused her and my family so much pain but it was now payback time. These were tears of joy in her eyes. The first of many.

On the Sunday morning I made my way down to St Mark's. I sat on the seat I had been used to filling on the left-hand side about four rows from the front. Some of my pals came and congratulated me on finishing the programme. This felt so good. I was beaming with a healthy sense of achievement. I joined with my church praising God and thanking Him for setting me free from my old life.

When I left Ireland to go to Teen Challenge there were no

regular workers from St Mark's out on the streets in Dublin. I was concerned that there might still be none, but to my delight I discovered that there was now a couple involved in the church, Alan and Barbara Sweetman, who had big hearts to reach out to the addicts on the streets. Since that time they have paved the way for many addicts and their families to come to freedom and have never failed to acknowledge and support those who return from rehabilitation. Alan and Barbara have made great strides in this work and have built up others in the church to reach out with them. They now have a beautiful women's centre in Ireland where God's work of bringing many to freedom has begun.

Chapter Twenty
The High Call of God

I spent several days with my family before returning to Wales. I worked in the Teen Challenge Centre as a volunteer for a while. Then I received an invitation from an American mission in London called Victory Outreach to work on the same streets that I used to sleep rough on. I spoke to John Macey, the director of Teen Challenge about it and he gave me his blessing, so I travelled to London in June of 1992 and lived at 195 King's Cross Road. Victory Outreach had offered me a bed free of charge in this crumbling old house in the middle of the red light district of London. I travelled by train to Euston station and arrived late, at about 10 p.m. Memories of my first visit to London came back to me. Most of the problems that I had brought to London with me the first time were now gone and in their place was a deep desire to tell as many hurting people as I could about the love of God.

I walked through the streets that I used to sleep on and tears trickled down my face as memories flooded back. I wasn't prepared for this sudden rush of memories of so much pain, hurt, abuse and hopelessness. "My God, it's a miracle that I'm still alive," I said aloud to myself. I then got on the Underground, taking the time to enjoy paying my way now and not jumping the barriers, as had been my wont. I got off the Tube train and came up the huge escalator to come out at King's Cross.

The sound of hundreds of cars with their accompanying acrid fumes met me: horns beeping, taxi doors clicking open and banging shut, people running for trains, others shouting for taxis. Shop lights and streetlights made it seem like daytime at night. Most people passing by on their way to catch a train only see the Cross, as it's called, in a passing commuter dimension. They cannot or do not want to see the dimension of human suffering that is just beyond the hundreds of other commuters coming and going. I, on the other hand, only noticed the commuters as I made myself focus on them. The dimension of the fourth world, the world of the addicted, the alcoholic, the beggar and homeless is what I more readily saw and felt. King's Cross is the bottom of the barrel as far as addiction is concerned, yet I was still at home there, I knew my way around, people acknowledged me as I went past. It was as if they recognised me although I had never met these hurting people before. I felt like I knew them all intimately; there was an identification that bypassed my recovery. God had allowed me to keep my passport to the streets. I had earned the right to live in the fourth world or to visit it whenever I wanted. I respected these people, because I knew where they were at.

One old tramp looked at me. I went up to him and held my hand out, saying "Hey! How's it goin'?" I looked straight into his eyes as his gaze caught mine and didn't say anything else. I just held his hand tight and looked at him. Then I prayed quietly, but loud enough for him to hear me. "Oh God, bless my friend, put a song in his heart and keep him well." Tears welled up in his eyes, streaming down his cheeks; that holy sense of the presence of God came, and I hugged him. I put my arms around his smelly body and told him that I would be living at 195 King's Cross Road if he ever needed me. I left him then and continued the 200-yard walk to my new home. I was half-way there when a fight broke out across the road from me. I saw the blade of a knife flash as it was plunged into the neck of a man and then the blood spurting from his neck; a voice shouted, "Someone get an ambulance!" There was another scuffle as someone tried to stop the man with the knife from running away. I slipped into a phone box and dialled 999. "The ambulance will be there shortly," I was told. I then went on my way – you didn't interfere in those kinds of fights. I reached 195 King's Cross Road without any further incidents.

THE HIGH CALL OF GOD

I knocked on the blue door, stood back and waited. I could see two drug addicts injecting themselves in the four-foot-wide walkway that was at the side of my new home.

The door opened and a big man was standing there looking at me. He had black hair and a big moustache.

"Hey – you must be Jonathon Edwards," he said.

"*John* Edwards," I replied, "my name is John Edwards."

"Come on in, John," the big guy said, speaking with a strange American accent. "My name is Art. Welcome to our home. Come on and I'll show you your room. You will be sharing with a guy called Stephen."

I had heard about Art. He had been an assassin with the Mexican Mafia, but had become a Christian while he was on death row in San Quentin prison. I had heard that after a long court case he had been released and he now worked on the streets of London helping people.

Art and I got on very well. We shared with each other how our lives had been changed since we became Christians. We became good friends, enjoying many a good laugh and many an experience on the streets. I met the other three workers in the house: Steven, Paul and Peter. They were all former addicts who had experienced God in ways similar to me. I spent about six months living in King's Cross with them.

Each day I went on the streets. I had hundreds of incredible experiences. I got to know many of the tramps, alcoholics, addicts and prostitutes. Each Thursday we would open up the ground floor of 195 King's Cross Road to feed, clothe and help these hurting people in whatever way we could. I got to know many people quite well and was able to have a big influence on their lives.

One day someone started a fight with the alcoholic tramps. These men and women used to visit me regularly to talk, laugh, cry, eat or just sit. Occasionally they would ask me to pray with them.

"Will Jesus save us, John?" they would ask me.

"Of course He will," I'd answer. "He will also give you eternal accommodation. You will never be homeless again."

Often they would pray to ask God to forgive them of their

sins and come into their lives. Again and again that lovely holy sense of the presence of God would come and touch these lovely people. Benny was one of these lads. He was a chronic alcoholic. He often tried to stop drinking but could not. During the fight that day someone knocked him to the ground and jumped on his head a couple of times. He went unconscious but woke up shortly afterwards, complaining of a headache. He went up to the park where he and his pals used to drink and sleep. Benny went to sleep that night under the usual big tree, his girlfriend, also a tramp and alcoholic, sleeping by his side. Benny never woke up; he died in his sleep.

The next morning seven or eight of the tramps came round to me at 195. All of them were very upset as they told me about Benny. "John," they said, "we didn't drink this morning, none of us. We've kept all the money we have to go towards buying some flowers for Benny. We wondered if you would come up to the park with us and pray at the spot where Benny died."

The lads had only 50 pence for the flowers. My friends in 195 and I bought a few white roses and together we went to the park. We placed the white roses on the spot where Benny had died. We then stood in a circle and held hands. We thanked God for Benny's life and prayed for his family, wherever they were. I then prayed for all the tramps and asked God to protect them and lead them to freedom. After that we sat for a while and talked. We reminisced about Benny's life, laughing about the funny situations he had got into and feeling sad about the way he had died. Several of them were beginning to shake quite badly because they had not had their drink that morning. Being sensitive to this, I said, "Well, we all have business to do, so I'll see you all later." I stood up to leave, but before I could go, Barry, the ringleader, came up to me and shook my hand. "Thanks, John," he said. "You give us hope that even we can make it." In turn all the tramps came to me and shook my hand. I had a lump in my throat when I left the park that morning.

I wish that people would realise that everything they own, houses, cars, money, jobs, family are added on to an otherwise homeless life. Most people are only three or four pay cheques

THE HIGH CALL OF GOD

from being penniless and homeless.

Miracles on the Streets

Many may think that going back to the streets was a crazy thing to do, but for me it was the high call of God. There is no better place on earth than the streets; you meet real people, honest people who have nothing to lose or prove. Like the time when I was walking through Leicester Square in London. It was a cold night and the ground was wet. The whole world was passing through this place. It is only a couple of hundred yards from Piccadilly Circus. There were Chinese, Japanese, Germans, French, Australian, Americans and people from every other nation that you could think of passing by that night. The rich and poor, black, white, brown and yellow rubbed shoulders as they passed through this crossroads of the world. In the middle of all this I came across a drunken tramp that was lying on the ground just outside one of the cinemas. The rain had not diluted the blood that was caked and dried into his face; the white cartilage on his broken nose showing through and the smell of excrement filling the air around him. The telltale sign of diarrhoea showing brown on his old white trainers confirmed the fact that he had soiled himself. I knelt down on the ground beside him to see if he was breathing, feeling sick from the stench as I did so. He was OK apart from being in a drunken sleep. I tried to wake him but he was out for the count. I put a note in his pocket with my address on it and a prayer for him to read whenever he came to. I then put my hands on him and prayed, "Please, God, help this man and give him hope for the future. He is without hope unless you help him. God, please become real to him, just as you are to me."

I left him and made my way down to Charing Cross. I had begun to sleep out on the streets in order to meet the homeless and addicted. I brought an old sleeping bag for the night and £2.50 to feed myself. I didn't allow myself more than the average homeless person had to live on. Before settling down I went into Charing Cross station to call a friend and let them know that I was safe. I was just finishing the phone call and putting down the receiver when who should walk around the corner but the tramp with the broken nose that I had prayed for thirty minutes earlier. I was amazed. He had no idea that I had prayed for him and out of the nine million or so people in London he walked right up to me. I whispered to myself, "This is a miracle happening."

"Excuse me," he said, with a husky voice, "could you do me a favour?"

"What is that?" I asked him.

"Could you go into that shop there and buy me a can of cider? They won't serve me and I need a drink." I studied his face as he spoke to me. It was scarred from many fights and falls, his brown hair was unkempt, his beard was too long and had bits of food stuck in it just below his lip and on his moustache. But the thing I noticed about him more than anything else was the sadness: the lack of love and the loneliness of his life, showing so clearly in his eyes. They were dead eyes that reflected only fear and hopelessness. Many of the homeless have this sad look about them. Right now this man needed a drink.

"I will, on one condition," I said.

"What's that?" he asked me.

"That you sit down with me for a while and talk to me."

He looked at me, no doubt surprised that I would spend time talking to him. "Right then," he said, "I will."

He gave me the little money he had, so I went into the off-licence and bought him a can of strong cider like he asked me to. I bought a can of Coca-Cola for myself from my own money.

"Let's sit over here on the ground," I said to the tramp, pointing to a corner of the station. We both sat down on the cold ground with our backs against the wall to drink and talk. He quickly opened the can of cider and took a long swig. Commuters passed by and looked at us with obvious distaste. They had no idea that a miracle was taking place. To the commuters we were the scum of the earth.

"My name's John," I said. "What's yours?"

"Josie," he answered between swigs of cider.

"You're Irish," I said to him.

"Yeah, I'm from Cork."

THE HIGH CALL OF GOD

"I'm from Dublin," I informed him. "Can I tell you a bit about myself, Josie?"

"Go ahead," he answered. I was aware that his cider was almost gone so I only had a few minutes to talk to him before he would be off to get more money for drink. I related to Josie in about five minutes a brief account of my life, how I had been alcoholic, how I had lived on the streets and how God had changed my life. I was amazed when he actually put down the can of cider between his knees to listen to me. He begun to hang onto every word that I was saying to him. He was looking straight into my eyes, firstly to see if I was telling the truth, I expect. Tramps know when people are lying.

"I was a Catholic, John," Josie said. "I don't go to chapel any more though, I feel too dirty." He then asked me a question, that both shocked and delighted me. "John, do you think that God would come into my life just like he has come into yours?"

"I know that He would, Josie," I answered. "Can I pray for you, Josie – the same prayer that I prayed when God came into my life?"

"Yeah, go ahead," he replied. I prayed that God would touch Josie's life; that He would give him a sense of His presence about him and that He would become real to him. I prayed something that I always pray for people on the streets – that God would put a song back in his heart and a skip in his step. Then I led Josie in what I call the sinner's prayer. I said the words and Josie prayed the words after me.

The world continued to pass us by as we two new friends prayed before the King of kings. The smell of excrement was awful. People turned away in disgust at the smell coming from us. Yet that holy hush of the unmistakable and majestic presence of God joined Josie and me as we prayed.

"Dear Lord God," I prayed, and Josie repeated the words after me. "I believe that Jesus is the Son of God; that He died and shed His blood for the forgiveness of my sins; that on the third day He rose from the dead and is now in heaven having paid the price for my sins. Please, God, forgive me all my sins. I give you my life. Now please come into me and give me eternal life, in Jesus' name."

I then prayed the Lord's Prayer with Josie. He held his two hands together like an altar boy as I did so. He asked me to slow down so that he could repeat the words after me. "Our Father, who art in Heaven," I began, and Josie repeated the words as before, only this time with his hands together. "Our Father who art in heaven." I turned to look at him because the sincerity in his voice touched me. Tears were streaming down his face, coursing a way over the dried blood and into his dirty beard. "Hallowed be your name . . ." "Hallowed be your name . . ." We went through the whole prayer together. Then Josie looked at me. He had forgotten his can of cider now.

"John, that was lovely praying that. I can feel a lovely feeling inside me. What's that?"

"That is God touching you, Josie," I answered.

"Let's pray the Our Father again," he said. So off we went again, "Our Father who art in Heaven" and so on. When we had finished praying, Josie looked at me and said, "Thanks John, I'll never forget you." I looked at him; his haggard, scarred face still caked in blood, the cartilage still showing through his twisted nose, which had obviously been broken more than once. The dirt was still on his face and beard and yet there was something different about him. His eyes were not dead any more; instead, there was a glint in them, a glint of life; hope had come through a meeting with God. I knew then that Josie would never be the same again.

Josie and I talked for another while. He said that he was going over to Euston Station Superloo for a bath. I gave him several different addresses where he could get help. I then gave him my last few pence as he left. He shook my hand before he went. I tell you, a handshake from Josie that night could not be matched by that of the richest person in the entire world – or even of the Queen of England!

My eyes followed him as he left Charing Cross Station, his trainers covered in excrement, his trousers hanging heavy at the back because he had dirtied himself. He still stank and people looked at him as if he were the scum of the earth. Yet there was a slight skip in his step now. "Thank you for Josie,

God, and thank you for my life – it's been well worth it."

I was hungry now and I had no money left. I picked up my sleeping bag, intending to head for a doorway where I planned to meet some more homeless people. "God, I could do with some food before I go to bed," I silently prayed. I stepped outside the station and as I did so a red van pulled up and a lovely West Indian woman jumped out. Looking at me she said, "Would you like a cup of tea?"

"I'd love one," I laughingly answered.

"Are you hungry?" she said.

"I'm hungry," I replied, still laughing.

"What's so funny?" she asked, with a smile on her face.

"Oh nothing, it's a private joke between me and God," I said.

"Well, I have some homemade chilli con carne in the van if you want some."

"Yes, please."

She heaped a paper plate with the most beautiful chilli con carne I had ever tasted. Then, armed with my tea, chilli and fresh bread with real butter, I headed for my doorway. I didn't sleep in just any doorway in those post-Teen Challenge days; I now slept in the plush doorway of the Adelphi Theatre. I climbed into my sleeping bag, pulled it up around me and watched the wealthy and the wise pass me by as they left the theatre. Some looked scornfully at me. One kind lady offered me a pound coin.

"Thank you – that is very kind of you, ma'am," I said. "But to tell you the truth, I have everything I need."

I would sometimes spend up to three or four days going round the streets. I would visit Cardboard City and other places that I used to frequent, speaking to the homeless, addicted and destitute. My life of addiction more than qualified me for this work. I was so grateful to God. I could fill a book with the number of amazing experiences with street people that I had. Life was so good.

Mafia Miracle in America

My mother was unwell during this time and I was planning to go home and spend some special time with her and my family. Just before I returned to Ireland, however, I was invited to visit

America with Art. There was a Victory Outreach conference being organised in San Diego for former addicts, gangsters and criminals. "They are all Christians now, John," Art said. "There will be about three-and-a-half thousand of us meeting together to thank God for our lives. It would be good for you to go." Art told me he would fix up some venues for us to tell our life stories together. Within the space of a few weeks I had my passport, a visa and my plane ticket to go to California. I was very much looking forward to seeing the States. Then in September of 1992 we headed for Los Angeles.

Art had arranged for us to stay with some of his friends at La Puente in LA. While I was there he suggested that we try to get in touch with the Don of the Mexican Mafia, the man who had taught Art everything in his Mafia days. Ernest Kilroy was his name. We managed to meet with him. He was an elderly but fit-looking man who had spent many years in prison. He was not a big man, yet he commanded a certain respect and carried an air of authority that made you know you didn't want to mess with him. We asked him to come to the conference in San Diego. He agreed to come but told us that the police probably wouldn't let him leave LA. We went to see the parole board and after we agreed to meet certain conditions they allowed Ernest to come to the conference.

We travelled the two-and-a-half-hour journey to San Diego together and booked into a hotel when we arrived. The next morning we headed for the conference centre. Outside the huge centre were dozens of Harley Davidson motorbikes, all belonging to former Hell's Angels who were now Christians. We walked into the auditorium and there we saw hundreds of former addicts, many of them scarred and tattooed.

The meetings themselves were an experience that I will never forget, with three-and-a-half thousand of us thanking God, singing worship songs and praying. It was unbelievable. Each day Ernest sat with Art and I and listened to the speakers but the hard, sometimes evil look in his eyes never left. On the second last night of the conference a Mexican woman got up and told her story about how God had changed her life. At some point in her talk she said, "La M., the Mexican Mafia killed my brother in a drive-by shooting. I know there are Mafia people in here." Ernest's body stiffened and he listened with increased attention. The woman continued.

"I want the Mafia people who are here to know that I forgive them for what they did to my brother, because I know that God has forgiven me for the evil things I have done in my life."

As soon as he heard those words Ernest fell from his seat beside me unto his knees. He began to cry and ask God to forgive him for all he had done wrong in his life. He cried for the best part of two days. When he finally came around he was a different man. His eyes were different, the hardness and evil were gone. He was changed.

That night Ernest's wife Rosa came down to meet us and Art arranged for us to meet with some other friends of his, Blinky Rodriguez and his wife Anna. They were kickboxing champions who ran a Christian Kickboxing club. I laughed when I heard this. "Only in America," I thought. We arranged to meet in LA the following night for a meal. Art spent a lot of time talking to Ernest during that day, explaining the gospel to him and the Christian way of life. When night fell we met in a Mexican restaurant near Hollywood in Los Angeles. I was amazed at the company I was in. I joked that I was in worse company now than I used to be in when I was an addict. We laughed a lot that night and rejoiced at what God was doing.

Ernest left the Mafia shortly afterwards; he and his wife had their marriage blessed and they began a new life as Christians. The last I heard, several of the leaders of the Mafia had left and were now Christians. Ernest, Art and others were sharing with thousands of gang members about the love of God, and many were coming to faith in Christ.

Before I left the States I had the privilege of telling my life story in the 3,000-strong church belonging to Victory Outreach.

Chapter Twenty-One
I'm On Top of the World Ma

A short time later I returned to Ireland as I had planned, just to spend some quality time with my mother and the rest of the family. It was really special getting to know them again. I had many amends to make, and I discovered that it takes time to rebuild trust. I had spent years abusing my family through my addiction. I had often heard of child abuse but now I realised that there is also family abuse. I had seriously hurt my brothers and sisters; I had made many promises to them and had let them down so often that now it would take time to build lasting trust. Once I realised this I put all my energy into rebuilding relationships.

I got myself a little flat and lived a fairly quiet life, spending time with my mam and brothers and sisters, just getting to know them again and enjoying their company. I loved bringing my mam out for meals or taking her to see her friends in their houses. We had many laughs together and our relationship was renewed. God was restoring the years I had lost through my addiction. During this time in Ireland I also went to see all the people that I owed money to from my old life, either by borrowing or through unlawful exploits. I really enjoyed paying off the debts to old acquaintances and to the shopkeepers whom I had bounced cheques with. The look on some of their faces was reward enough. They were amazed that I had changed enough to make amends where possible.

I spent almost a year back in Ireland. It was a good year but I had itchy feet again and needed a challenge. I felt ready to get involved in some kind of ministry work. There was still a lot of trouble in Northern Ireland at this time; people were being shot and destroyed by bombs and the violence was still causing much devastation in the lives of innocent people. I wanted to do something about it, so together with a few friends of mine I arranged a prayer walk from Belfast to Dublin. We began it at the Shankhill Road in Belfast and spent five days walking to Dublin. This was the beginning of the walks that one day would bring me to many different countries around the world, preaching the gospel and helping many thousands of people.

Scotland

In early 1996 an opportunity arose for me to manage a rehabilitation centre on a little island just off the Ayrshire coast in Scotland called Cumbrae. The nearest mainland port was a half-mile away: a town called Largs. I had a sense of destiny in my inner being as I went to work in this lovely island. I knew that I had a lot of potential. There was a worldwide vision inside me that was screaming to be fulfilled. Yet, strange as it may seem, my self-esteem was very low and I lacked confidence. I knew that this time in Scotland would help me grow and mature into the person I desperately wanted to be.

I learned a lot about myself and about other people during my time working there. When off duty, I stayed in a nice one-bedroom flat in Largs on my own. Sometimes I would feel quite lonely. I didn't have many visitors and I was still getting used to this new life as a free man. I was often misunderstood and found it quite difficult to explain myself to others. I had a vision to take my walks around the world and to pray for addicts. I had an eye for business too; given the opportunity I could make a buck in almost any situation but I didn't have the experience to develop my business skills yet. I knew I could excel if I just had the right people around me, people who would help me develop in character and help me come to my full potential as an individual and as an evangelist.

My pals from Ireland who really knew me would come to visit on occasions. It was great to see them; we would talk till the early hours of the morning and laugh, pray and worship together. I loved them. The great thing about it was that most of them knew me from the days when I was addicted so they understood me and also believed in me. "John, you will take the Gospel around the world one day," they would say to me. "You are a great preacher, John, a natural." Some of my friends were very gifted singers and songwriters, while others were great preachers. God had touched us all powerfully. There was no jealousy or competition between us; just good fellowship, fun, encouragement and love. I needed their love and encouragement very much. After they had gone home I would feel lonely again. I longed for a friend, a companion, a soul-mate that would understand and love me for who I was; someone who would recognise the potential in me and would help me develop as a man.

I began to pray that God would give me a wife. I had come to a place in my life where I was willing to serve God and stay single if that is what He wanted, but now this desire for companionship, friendship and love got stronger and stronger. I was forty years of age and time was passing quickly for me.

I had read in a book that when we pray we would need to be specific. The book said to write down every detail that was required. This sounded a bit odd but I didn't know what else to do so I wrote down twenty-one qualities that I desired in my new wife. In faith I prayed for a Christian woman who has "big eyes, a nice smile, is gentle, likes holding my hand and cuddling, even in public; a woman who recognises my potential and is 100 percent for me. She should have fair hair and be not more than five foot six inches in height. She also should not be a former addict or alcoholic."

The list went on and on until I had twenty-one details on it. I wrote them all in my journal and then I began to pray for them. I must admit I felt a bit guilty, even presumptuous, as I prayed for them. As was my habit, I began every day in prayer, only now I added my very special request. I would say, "Lord, you stated in the book of Genesis that it is not good for a man to be alone. Please send me the woman that I believe you have for me." Over a period of several months I prayed in this way, yet there was no sign of an answer coming along. I kept praying, though – "Lord, please; I believe that you want me to be married and that you want me to have the wife of my dreams. Please lead me to her." I honestly believed that God would answer this prayer.

Business as *Un*usual!

Saturday was my day off and most weeks I would set off in my car to Glasgow, spend the day there walking around, or visiting the Christian book shop and the famous "Barrowlands" markets to try to pick up a bargain or two. One Saturday in the middle of 1996 I set off as usual for Glasgow. It was a nice day, a bit overcast, but pleasant; nothing to write home about, no clue or hint that my life was once again about to change for the good. I got in my car and headed towards the main Glasgow Road. I had to go through Largs to get to this road. I drove as usual through the town, past the bakery, down the hill, turning left by the hardware shop, past the little Nazarene church on my right and then past Woolworth's on my left. Suddenly I heard God speak to me. There was the holy hush that usually accompanied God's voice when I experienced it; that same voice that I had learned to listen for was now speaking to me again. "Turn your car around and go into the Nazarene Church." That was all God said, but I knew that I must be obedient to this direction. I knew from experience that there was probably a miracle waiting to happen at the church.

My heart began to pound with anticipation. Who was I going to meet and what was going to happen? These and other questions flooded my mind. I loved situations like this. I came to the end of the road, indicated right and when the road was clear I did a U-turn and drove back to the little Nazarene church building. I parked my car about twenty feet away and getting out of the car I walked straight towards the front door of the church. People everywhere were going about their business, not paying any attention to me. I remember thinking that it was such a privilege to be a real Christian: no day was just another day, business as usual; for me it was always business as unusual.

I'M ON TOP OF THE WORLD MA

I had no idea if the church door would be unlocked or if anyone would be there, but when I arrived I spotted a sign advertising the "Coffee Morning" that was taking place right at that moment. "Oh, well, if nothing else I will get a cup of coffee," I mused, and pulling open the door of the church I stepped in. In the sanctuary, tables had been laid for the event and about ten people were already seated. I put my hand in my pocket to get some money to pay for a coffee and to my horror I realised that I had left my money back in my flat. "Oh no! What am I going to do?" I felt like an idiot as I stood there surrounded by little old ladies and men who were sipping tea and eating cream cakes. I noticed a bookshelf on the wall nearest me and to conceal my confusion I picked up a book and began leafing through it. "God, please help me," I prayed mentally, "I am in here because I thought you wanted me to come in. Why am I in here, God?" I repeated this several times as I leafed through the book. I wasn't reading the words – I was panicking. "Oh God, why do you always seem to wait until I am in danger of looking silly, or until I almost panic, before you do something?"

"Excuse me sir, can I help you?"

"Eh, what?" I wasn't expecting anyone to speak to me at that moment.

"Are you all right, sir?" a girl asked me. "Can I get you anything to drink? A cup of coffee maybe, or tea?"

"Oh, hello! Sorry, you startled me," I replied. "I was engrossed in the book."

"Would you like something to drink?" she repeated.

"Well, I am a little embarrassed," I replied. "I intended to get a coffee but as I came in here I realised that I had left my money at home."

"Don't worry about that," the girl said. "You sit down over there at that corner table and I'll get you a cup of coffee. It'll be on the house."

"Thank you," I replied.

"You can bring the book over with you and have a read of it if you like."

"What book? Oh this book," I said, realising that I still had it in my now sweaty hands. "Thanks; I will."

WALKING FREE

I sat down at my designated table. "God, I love these divine appointments, but what is going on here? Please tell me." No answer came; the heavens were like brass. "I am either a complete nutter," I thought, "or God is having a good laugh because He knows the outcome of this. If people knew what I was doing in here they would put me back in a psychiatric hospital." I chuckled to myself. Oh, what a blessed life to live. Even some Christians have not experienced this kind of adventure with God. I had butterflies of excitement in my tummy.

"Here's your cup of coffee, sir."

She had startled me again. "Oh! Thanks," I replied.

"Do you mind if I sit down for a minute? My name is Janet, and that's my wee pal-y wal-y Tricia in the kitchen down there. We are part of the team that run this coffee morning."

"Wee pal-y wal-y!" I thought to myself. "These Scots have some strange sayings."

"Tricia, come on down and meet this wee Irish man," Janet shouted, and everyone looked over to see the wee Irish man. *Wee pal-y wal-y* then came out of the kitchen and came down to meet the wee Irish man.

Tricia sat down beside Janet and they both asked me questions about Ireland and what I was working at in Scotland. I couldn't take my eyes off Tricia; she was so beautiful, with her big, amazing eyes. Her fair hair and lovely smile especially caught my attention – and then, she was so gentle! "Man," I said to myself, "this lady is like an angel. She's lovely."

We chatted for quite a while, forgetting everyone else. If this "coffee morning" had been a commercial venture, Tricia and Janet would both have been fired for lack of attention to the other customers.

The girls wanted to know more about the work that I was doing, so they invited me to attend their church on the following night, which was Sunday. I agreed to meet them and looked forward to it.

I left the Nazarene Church floating on air. I knew that something had happened between Tricia and I that morning. I am usually slow on the uptake with these matters, but that morning I knew that God had been working. He had begun something that I could not and did not want to stop. In fact, I have learned since that no one can stop what God begins.

The next night was a long time coming. I met Tricia and Janet again, of course, and they introduced me to their pastor, a lovely man of God called Fred Cowan. Later, Tricia shared with me that she had been married before but had been divorced about twelve years previously. She had four children, all of whom except one were still teenagers. Trish and I began to see each other on a friendship level and during the following year I got to know her children, Kevin, Paul, Leanne and Amanda. They were lovely: fine examples of the love and discipline that Tricia had put into them. I became a friend to them and enjoyed going around to their house.

As time passed by, I knew that I was falling in love with Tricia. She had everything that I needed in a woman, and more. Bur how was I to tell her? I was very shy about such things.

Paul is Tricia's second eldest son. At that time he had applied for a job in England, and although Tricia was happy when his application was successful, she was quite upset that he was leaving home, particularly as he was the first to go. On the morning of his departure, she was crying and I asked her if she would like to go to Loch Lomond with me for the rest of the day, hoping to cheer her up. I also hoped that day to ask her to go out with me as my girlfriend. I was in love, I wanted to marry her, but I just didn't know how to tell her. We had not so much as held hands or kissed yet.

Chapter Twenty-Two
A Divine Romance

We set off early and I was a nervous wreck. I am sure Tricia had no idea of the suffering I went through that day. We had lunch in the lovely town of Luss by the loch. I tried to work up the courage to ask her then but I couldn't. I then tried to ask her at the kilt-makers we visited. The setting was perfect; a gentle stream flowed in the garden, we sat and talked on a lovely fallen tree, ducks quacked and waddled about . . . Tricia was relaxed and enjoying the day, while I was uptight and nervous.

"Are you OK, John?" she asked me several times.

"Yes, I'm fine," I lied in return. *Oh God, help me to ask her, Pleeeaaaase*. No go, I just couldn't do it. We went through the whole day like that, Tricia really enjoying herself while I was suffering from nervous exhaustion by the end of it. I drove all the way home without asking the all-important question. We sat for a while outside her house but I just couldn't do it.

I felt so silly; I was 41 years of age and I couldn't ask a girl out! "John Edwards, you're hopeless," I kept telling myself.

"I'd better be going in now, John," Tricia said.

"OK," I answered. Tricia put her hand on the car door and was about to get out when I almost shouted, *"Wait!"*

"What is it, John?" she asked.

"Well, you know that I was offered a job in Sunderland as an evangelist in a church?"

"Do you mean the one where there was a house with the job, John?" I could see that she thought I was leading up to telling her I was going away, and this flustered me even more, so much so that my stutter came back briefly.

"Y-y-yes, that one; b-b-but I was only wanting to tell you that . . ." *Oh God, I'm making a mess of this.* " . . . I am not taking the job. You see . . ." *Sweat was now pouring down my back; I was losing weight with the strain of coming to the point. And then I went ahead and blew it big time. Instead of asking her to be my girlfriend, I blurted out:* "You see Tricia, I, I love you and I want to marry you; will you marry me?"

Milliseconds passed. I only meant to ask her to be my girlfriend, and now I was sure that I had frightened her off. I anxiously read her face and body language for signs of rejection. The world seemed to be turning in slow motion. That moment would definitely remain with me for ever.

Then a big smile spread across Tricia's lovely face. *She's going to laugh at me, I thought.* And then her eyes filled with tears. What – have I upset her? *Oh God, help me here . . .*

"John Edwards, I have loved you since I met you, and I would love to be your wife. Of course I'll marry you."

Oh! Fireworks went off in my head! This was incredible – Tricia loved me! We had not so much as held hands or kissed until then, but now for the first time we held each other in a loving embrace, full of gratitude to God. It was a wonderful, special moment.

A knock on the car window brought us to our senses. It was Kevin, Tricia's eldest son. "Mum, I'm just going down to Ryan's house, I'll be back later – is that OK?" I was reminded that I would also have a lovely family when we got married. Life was so good.

All our relations and friends were so happy for us; our phones never stopped ringing and lots of letters came, full of congratulations. We planned our wedding day, setting the date for the 20th September 1997, the tenth anniversary of my salvation. We invited 200 people and both the service and the celebrations were to take place in St Mark's, my home church in Dublin. I was living by faith, with no visible income at all, yet we planned a beautiful wedding that could have cost thousands of pounds. Tricia and I prayed one night at about eleven o'clock that God would provide for us and He did, in so many ways. For example, Trish's family lived in Donegal on the north west coast of Ireland and on one occasion both she and I wanted to come to Ireland and visit our families, but we were lacking the necessary funds. This was the same time we needed the money for an engagement ring. So one night we prayed, making both requests. The very next morning, only eight hours after we had prayed, a friend of ours, who knew nothing about our need, woke up with the thought of giving us a sum of money. She believed it was God speaking to her so in obedience she came around and gave us the money. It was enough to buy the ring that Tricia wanted and to visit our families in Ireland.

I also visited Ireland several times, alone, to meet with my friends, Brian and Ann Kelly. They were to cook the food and help arrange everything for the day. They were a fantastic encouragement, especially when they knew that I was doing all the arranging by faith. One night while we were planning the four-course menu for the wedding, they asked me, "How much money do you have to put towards this, John?"

"Nothing at all," I answered. "God *will* provide."

"I was afraid you were going to say that," Brian said, laughing. Then he added, "We know God and you well enough to believe that God will provide."

Tricia is a dressmaker and she was busy making her own wedding dress, but, of course, I was not allowed to see it at all. I would call round sometimes and she would be busy working on it in her workroom. I would hear her friends talking about Tricia sewing, by hand, lots of pearls and sequins onto her dress.

God provided everything for us. Paul was to give his mum away in place of her father Francie, who had passed on a couple of years beforehand. He was a man I would love to have met; he is still spoken of so highly by Tricia's mum and the rest of her family, and others who knew him.

My friend Shay Phelan was to be Best Man, with my brother Eamon as Groom's Man; Janet, Tricia's *Pal-y wal-y* was Chief Bridesmaid, and Leanne and Amanda were Bridesmaids also.

WALKING FREE

All the Scottish men and I wore kilts with the Flower of Scotland tartan. Maire Brennan, the voice of Clannad and fellow-worshipper at St Mark's, agreed to sing and play harp for us at the wedding and Brenda Burrowes (now Rossman) was to be our worship leader. We had a full Celtic band organised to play Christian worship music, with both harp and uilleann pipes featured. A friend arranged for an Irish army band member to play the bagpipes for us as we arrived. His name was Michael Jackson – yes, all the big names were there! But there was one name that I had especially prayed would show up. His invitation was printed on the front of every wedding service sheet. It said: *Jesus also was invited to the wedding feast.* I was desperate for his presence to be felt at our wedding service.

We travelled to Ireland a couple of days before the wedding to facilitate rehearsals and put final touches to the preparations for the day. All our Irish friends gathered round us to help in whatever way they could. The church was beautifully decorated with lots of exotic flowers; soft cream drapes covered the balconies, candles on stands stood on the plush red carpet. Candles lined the aisle, ready to light the way for my bride.

I had one important appointment before the wedding took place. Tricia and I travelled up to the graveyard at Howth where my father is buried. I went to the spot where my father's grave is, and cleaned the weeds and stray grass from the top of the grave as if I was brushing stray hair away from his face. I was fully conscious that there were only bones there now, but there were also so many memories buried with him. I knew that he would be happy for me if he were alive and also very proud. "Da," I said, as I pulled Tricia to my side at the foot of the grave. "Meet Tricia, my fiancée. We are to be married tomorrow."

We stood there for a while, burying the past, letting go of hurts and failures. When we left the grave I felt as if we had my father's blessing.

The night before the wedding arrived, and I felt so excited inside. Everything was ready; God had provided all we needed.

A DIVINE ROMANCE

I stayed with my friend Shay Phelan in his flat, along with two other friends, Terry Munnelly and Mike Brown, a black gospel singer from the States. We did not have a traditional "stag" night; my one wish at this wedding was to honour God, so there would be no alcohol at all. The toasts would be drunk with non-alcoholic wine. Tricia and the rest of the family stayed at our friends Alan and Barbara Sweetman's house. By all accounts they had a wildly exciting time. I heard later that the shower had broken and they had to visit a neighbour to finish off their showering.

Chapter Twenty-Three
Made in Heaven, Our Wedding Day

We laughed a lot while we got ready on the wedding morning, Mike Brown with his mad sense of humour bantering Terry and I as we tried to put our kilts on. Shay cooked a traditional Irish wedding breakfast for us and we sat chatting and eating in as relaxed a manner as possible. Shay's sister Ann was there too, she had just returned from Spain where she was now living. She ran around after us cleaning up our mess and turning out the lights after me. It was good to have that special woman's touch – she made sure that we were looking just right. Then the time to go to the church arrived. We all stood and prayed before we left the flat; we four men stood and prayed, "Lord, please bless this day with your presence and bless the marriage." We prayed for Tricia and the family that all would be well with them as they prepared. Then we headed off for the church, punctually chauffeured by Peter Barron, another friend from St Mark's.

Everyone was buzzing when we arrived. I looked great in my kilt, even if I say so myself, with the long, plaid cloak hanging over my shoulder and reaching down to the back of my knees. I stood at the front row with Shay and Eamon by my side. Pastor Gary Davidson stood near us, waiting to start, while in the seats where she sat with my brothers and sisters my ma was crying already. There were all my nieces and nephews – and there was Auntie Eileen, who had said that she wanted to live long enough to see me get married. She was in her 80s now. Almost every person that had played a significant part in my life was there – including the men who helped me when I first became a Christian. Friends from Scotland and Wales had arrived, and of course Tricia's mother Cathleen and many of her brothers and sisters were there as well. The church looked absolutely beautiful. I was so grateful to everyone who had helped out and felt privileged to have such good friends.

Gary informed me that Tricia was going to arrive in a few minutes. Shay and I stood up and I glanced over my shoulder at my family. There were Evelyn, Maeve, Geraldine, Eamon and Michael – only Pauline, who was still living in Portugal, had not been able to make it. My mother had such a happy look on her face and as she saw me looking at her she smiled. I felt time stand still; that smile said so much to me – it would take all the books in the world to even attempt to capture what was communicated through it. She was old now but I could see my ma at every stage in my life, always there, always loving me, never giving in. I am sure I must have put years on her through worry, pain and sadness. I gave her a private nod and she nodded back to me. It was OK for my ma to let me go now; Tricia was coming in to love me and be my wife. My ma knew that she couldn't hand me over to a better person than Tricia.

The bagpipes began to play in the churchyard and we could hear the haunting strains of the old hymn, "Amazing Grace" wafting in from outside. This was the signal that Tricia was entering the building.

At the end of the hymn the Celtic band broke into a beautiful tune that spoke of *Jesus, Holy and Anointed One*. I knew that Tricia was now at the back door of the sanctuary, and after waiting a moment I glanced over my left shoulder to catch a glimpse of her. There she was, resplendent in her ivory wedding dress, looking absolutely stunning. The presence of God filled the church; God in His faithfulness had come to our marriage ceremony.

Tricia walked slowly down the aisle, all eyes fixed on her. She was beautiful and her face shone with happiness. She stood near my side and I took a step towards her. Pastor Gary led us in our wedding vows. Tricia and I looked into each other's eyes as, one after the other, we said, "I do". Then Gary spoke the familiar words, "I now pronounce you man and wife. You may kiss the bride." Everyone there went nuts at this time, cheering loudly. Maire Brennan and Brenda then sang the beautiful old hymn, "Be Thou My Vision", in Gaelic, after which Mike Brown stood up to sing for us. He was in a black jacket with a row of diamantes on each cuff and they sparkled as he sang "How Great Thou Art". Tears streamed down his black shiny face; I believe that he and everyone else experienced a touch of heaven as Christ walked amongst us.

Trish and I were now united in the presence of God. The pain was over; the joy was just beginning.

Epilogue

Nine long but very eventful years have passed since I wrote Walking Free. What a rollercoaster ride it has been, Tricia and I have been married for almost thirteen years now and we have been through some great heights and several lows during that time. We now live near Bradford in West Yorkshire.

We are happily married, have three gorgeous grandchildren. Amanda has two lovely boys, Antony and Darren, they are six and seven years old and they live near us. Kevin has a lovely little boy called Jonah, and he is six. They still live in Ayrshire, Scotland. Being a Grandparent or 'Gran and Papa' as they call us is wonderful, this has brought a brand new and fabulous dimension to our lives, one that we would not be without. I never thought I would have children in my life. God has been so gracious to us.

We have set up three rehabilitation centres in Scotland, one a girls centre and the other two men's centres. Many have been blessed and set free as a result of this work.

Tricia, myself and our team completed a prayer walk/cycle across America in 2005, all the way from Los Angeles to New York, millions heard the gospel through our testimonies as a result and were touched by our ministry. Many miracles happened during this walk and our faith was challenged like never before. The complete story of the walks is in my new book 'For Heavens Sake' This will be out soon.

I discovered I had Hepatitis C virus just after I finished that great walk, this had unfortunately turned into cancer by the time they found it. I then had to get a liver transplant. Imagine it, I walked/ cycled with my team all the way across America while I had cancer and Hepatitis C virus! God is amazing! That is an amazing story in itself. God worked miracles for us, if He hadn't I would not be here today to tell the story.

I retired from doing all ministry work for a while after my liver transplant, I handed over all the rehabs to our team in Scotland and they continue to do a great job. We attend and are involved in a fantastic church in Bradford, The Abundant life Church, which is led by Pastor Paul Scanlon. Walking Free Ministries is alive and well, we now have a centre called the 'Walking Free Centre' we hold discipleship classes and feed hungry and homeless people, we send addicts/alcoholics and other hurting people to rehab and help them in any way that we can. We often hold street sleeps, that is we sleep out with the homeless for up to three days, they come and stay with us on the streets, where we give them sleeping bags, provide warmth, food shelter, get hairdressers to do the street girls hair, provide portable showers, clothes and then hold a big banquet for them, it's fabulous. Hundreds of people, homeless and helpers join us. We will continue doing this from time to time. I have an amazing team who work tirelessly in reaching out to the lost and hurting of our world. Tricia and I believe the best is yet to come. We are now positioned for a great outpouring of God's provision, blessing and power to be released. It has been four years since my liver transplant, we are both well and now I am once again going out and about preaching the gospel and helping people, we are believing for great things for our future! We know it doesn't matter what happens to us in this life; we can be overcome by poverty, sickness, hard times, trials and tribulations yet they cannot stop us as long as we have the attitude that says, "I will not be beaten! I will not give up for I know that all things work together for the good of those who love God and who are called according to His purpose. The full story of my walks, battle with cancer, transplant operation and recovery and an incredible three hour visit to heaven(honestly) I had are in my new book 'For Heavens Sake' you can order it on our website www.walkingfree.org from January 2011.

So what's next for us?

EPILOGUE

Ireland

I have been desperate to do a work in Ireland since I left Teen Challenge, that is nearly 20 years ago. I tried on many occasions to go back home to work. I met with Christians, ministry leaders, with politicians, with funders for rehab, I walked the length and breadth of the country praying for God to move there, then I walked from Belfast to Dublin in 1993 praying for peace and revival. I believe God heard those prayers, but until now He has never opened the door or allowed me to go home to start a work. Each time I tried God would stop me and direct me to do something over in Britain, start a rehab, an outreach or other ministry. I have helped many Irish get into rehab in Britain, I've also reached out to help some of the parents in Ireland, I've even done a bit of outreach training here and there and preached in some churches, but no more than that. I am aware of the depth of problems Ireland has, with drug addiction, alcoholism, gangster and gang crime on the rise, I'm aware of the ridiculous and unbelievable sale of legal highs in head shops around the country. I have been informed that one of the graveyards in Dublin has been closed 20 years early as a direct result of young people dying from the consequences of addiction. This is a disgrace, the country and it's policies seem to be back to front.

I've longed to get back and work there, I am now delighted that doors have finally opened for us in both Northern and Southern Ireland. My old friend Liam Mc Namara and his lovely wife Mary have invited me to undertake ministry project work with their ministry, 'Vision For Revival' in Ireland. I am so excited by this, The vision that burns in their hearts is just the same as mine.

I believe this next season will be one of the greatest in our lives to date. Liam and Mary have a huge vision to bring revival to Ireland , reaching in to schools, prisons, churches, they have already begun to teach and train people in the work of outreach. This vision has burned in their hearts for many years. Liam was involved in the Full Gospel businessmen's Fellowship International, in fact Liam was one of the men who was involved with them when I had my encounter with God 23 years ago. Liam and Mary have developed a network of support for ministries, or fires, as they call them throughout Ireland and are committed to work with them developing unity, purpose and vision.

Now In the meantime I wish you well, I pray that God would bless you indeed, that He would protect you from evil and reveal Himself to you, that He would put a smile back into the hearts of us all.

If my book has touched your life and if you, like I have done would like to invite Jesus Christ into your life you can do so by praying sincerely this prayer.

Dear Jesus,

I believe you are the Son of God, I believe you died and shed your blood so as my sin's could be forgiven. I admit I am a sinner, I have done many things wrong, I have hurt people and I too have been hurt by others. I ask you to forgive me and I accept your forgiveness. Please come into my life, change me and make me like you. I promise that with your help I will change my ways. I give my life to you, please come into me by the power of your Holy Spirit. I receive you by faith. Thank you Jesus.

If you have sincerely prayed this prayer it would be very advisable and helpful for you to find a loving local bible believing church to go to. There are many around. Please contact us to let us know, we can then offer further help and direction to you if you need it. God bless. John

Walking Free Ministries

We are committed to reaching the lost, hurting and addicted of society, hundreds of people have been helped through our work but many more still need to be reached.

Walking Free is committed to reach and help as many people as possible, through outreach, teaching, training and with one to one ministry. Many thousands of parents suffer as they watch their children struggle with addiction in all it's forms.

We aim to reach as many of these parents as possible, also their children and society in general with a life changing message filled with hope, salvation, healing and encouragement.

Book John to speak

If you would like John Edwards to speak at your church or meeting you could contact him at: contact@walkingfree.org

Other books by John

God Help, my child's on drugs

God Help, I am an addict.

For Heaven's sake. (part two of John's story)

The above books will be available soon

Check the website for details

www.walkingfree.org